OILWORK
NORTH SEA DIARIES

THIS BUOY MARKS THE LOCATION
OF THE PIPER ALPHA PLATFORM FROM
PIPER BRAVO

SUE JANE TAYLOR

Birlinn

First published in 2005 by
Birlinn Limited
West Newington House
10 Newington Road
Edinburgh EH9 1QS

www.birlinn.co.uk

ISBN10: 1 84158 427 4
ISBN13: 978 1 84158 4 27 0

British Library Cataloguing-in-Publication Data
A catalogue record for this book is available from the British Library

Designed by Grayscotland Ltd, Tain, Scotland www.grayscotland.com
Printed and bound by Graficas Santamaría S.A., Spain

CONTENTS

LOCATION MAP

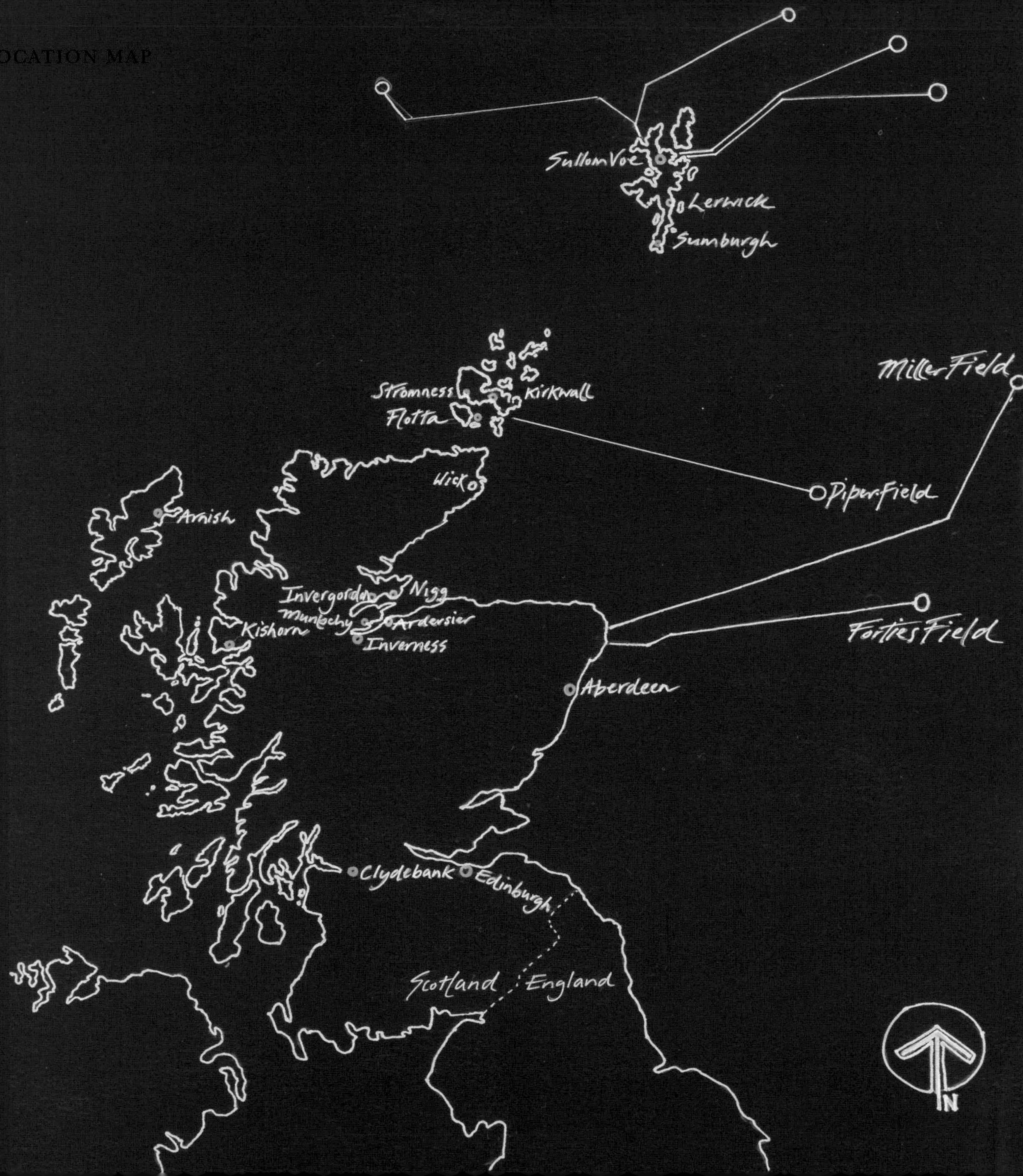

ACKNOWLEDGMENTS

Without the Stirling Shipping Company commission in 1984 my long journey into the world of North Sea oil would never have started. I would like to thank Gordon Bryce, my former printmaking lecturer at Grays, for putting my name forward, and Peter Wordie for his initiative in setting up the awards.

I am grateful to the public relations departments of all the oil companies and construction yards mentioned for allowing me access to their sites; particularly BP's Aberdeen office for enabling me to visit the Forties Field in 1986. I would also like to thank Alasdair and Lesley at UIE construction yard, and John Hood, Head Librarian at Clydebank Council, and his secretary Ann.

The period working on the Piper Alpha Memorial was a difficult time for me as it was for so many others. I will always be grateful to the Piper Outreach Social Work team and the Piper Alpha Families' Association for their support, especially survivors Bill Barron and Bob Ballantyne and their wives Trish and Pat, as well as Bob and Molly Pearston and Anne Gillanders, who sadly lost loved ones in the disaster. I would also like to thank Ronnie McDonald, Jake Malloy and Lorna Robertson at OILC for their constant encouragement and help; the Scottish Sculpture Workshop team; and Atlantis, John Purcell Paper, TN Lawrence, John Putman, J Smith & Sons and Ivo and Xanthe Mosley for helping promote my Oil Worker Scotland touring exhibition.

The preparation of this book has involved so many people that I apologise to anyone who has been missed. George Binette, Will Low, Miranda Melville, Liz Jones and Frances Walker initially urged me to pursue the project and Ian Westacott, my partner, has encouraged me continuously throughout. I am extremely grateful to John Edwards, Keeper of the Aberdeen Maritime Museum, who has faithfully supported my work and this book through its many phases as has Deidre Grant, Promotions Officer for Aberdeen City Council. Mary Beith, Dr Ronald Black and Lizzie MacGregor have been invaluable in sourcing poems, and my grateful thanks go to them and to George Gunn and the other poets who have kindly allowed me to use their work.

If it were not for Mary Unwin's cheerful ruthlessness and Pamela Willis's textual advice, editing more than a decade of diaries would have been a considerably longer task than it was. I am grateful to them both, as well as to Alison Munro and Melissa Gray, who have worked tirelessly on the book's publication and design. I would also like to thank Liz Short, Andrew Simmons and Hugh Andrew of Birlinn for their help through the publication process and Fin MacRae for photographing my work so sensitively.

I am grateful to CAN Offshore Ltd for letting me take over their board room to draw John Ellis, one of their Rope Access Technicians, and to Robert Zywietz for modelling the latest survival suit so well.

Without the assistance of Talisman Energy (UK) Ltd this book and its accompanying exhibition at the Aberdeen Maritime Museum may never have happened. I am extremely grateful to everyone in the Talisman team for their unflagging support and their generous funding of the final chapter which allowed me to revisit the Piper Field and lay so many ghosts to rest.

PREFACE

In 1984 I was one of twelve young Scottish art school graduates who were invited by Stirling Shipping Company, Glasgow, to create three artworks in the medium of 'print'. The chairman of Stirling Shipping, Peter Wordie, is a keen collector of contemporary art. He is also the son of geologist James Wordie, one of Shackleton's team in the 1914–17 Antarctic expedition. It was Wordie's vision to invite twelve artists to create works celebrating the company's tenth anniversary in the North Sea oil industry. Part of the brief was a journey offshore on one of their cargo supply vessels. Not all artists took up this invitation but instead visited the vessels in dock in Aberdeen harbour.

At the time I was studying in Stockholm and the company paid for my return flight to Aberdeen. It was a very dark, stormy December night when I boarded the *Stirling Teal* supply vessel on Pocra Pier, Aberdeen. In mostly 7/8 gale force weather, I spent a week tossed and turned about in an unknown world, a world of adventure and hardship, an all-male environment. Such was the visual stimulus that this became the genesis of my work on the North Sea oil industry from 1984–94. I returned to Sweden, working day and night on the images I had witnessed and recorded on paper. I received an award for my work and all the artists' works were exhibited throughout public galleries in Scotland.

Opposite Artist with Piper Alpha Memorial plaster originals, 1991.
PHOTO: RAY SMITH

Top Arnish construction yard, 1986.

Bottom From Stirling Albion's deck, looking up at the Miller Platform, 1988.

Looking up at Sante Fe 140 1984 colour etching

The Stirling Teal Boys 1984 colour etching

Aberdeen Harbour 1984 colour etching

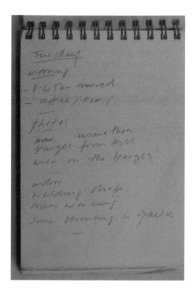
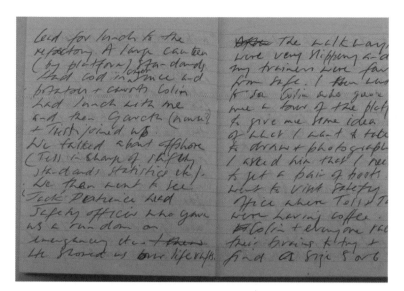
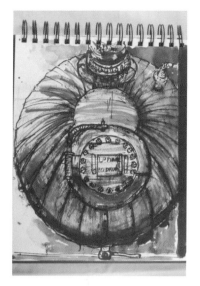

Above The artist used pocket-sized sketchbooks and diaries for immediate on-site observations.

I had always been aware of the oil industry in Scotland, it was part of contemporary Highland culture. I was born on the Black Isle and whilst growing up there in the 1970s the oil boom hit the Highlands of Scotland. Nigg and Ardersier construction yards flanked the Black Isle. I witnessed the radical changes to the area and the changes it made to peoples' lives there, both positive and negative. Some school classmates, many people from my village and even my own brother got careers in the industry. As an art student in Aberdeen, the oil capital of Europe, I was affected by its presence in the lack of cheap accommodation and the presence of leather jackets and overpowering aftershave in bars and nightclubs; guys walking down Union Street with cowboy boots usually two sizes too big for them. It never occurred to me that later in life I would spend over ten years doing intense work on this industry.

Gaining permission to visit oil-related sites was far from easy or straightforward: being a woman, an artist and wanting to draw on these sites were three major disadvantages. One advantage was living and working in London, where I was teaching at the Slade. I would phone up the oil companies' headquarters, which were always located in London, and ask for an appointment with the company director or public relations manager. Once the appointment was granted, half the battle was won. At the meeting I tried to convince them of the importance of my work. The fact that I had been granted a 'Glenfiddich Living Scotland Award' was of help here.

Most managers, 99 per cent of them men, were somewhat bemused by my mission. Plush London office quarters were a million miles away from the gritty, harsh conditions of the construction yards and oil terminals in the far north of Scotland and offshore in the North Sea; the Mediterranean was their idea of an artist's dream. But I was determined to get offshore and on to those oil-related sites, and that determination won through.

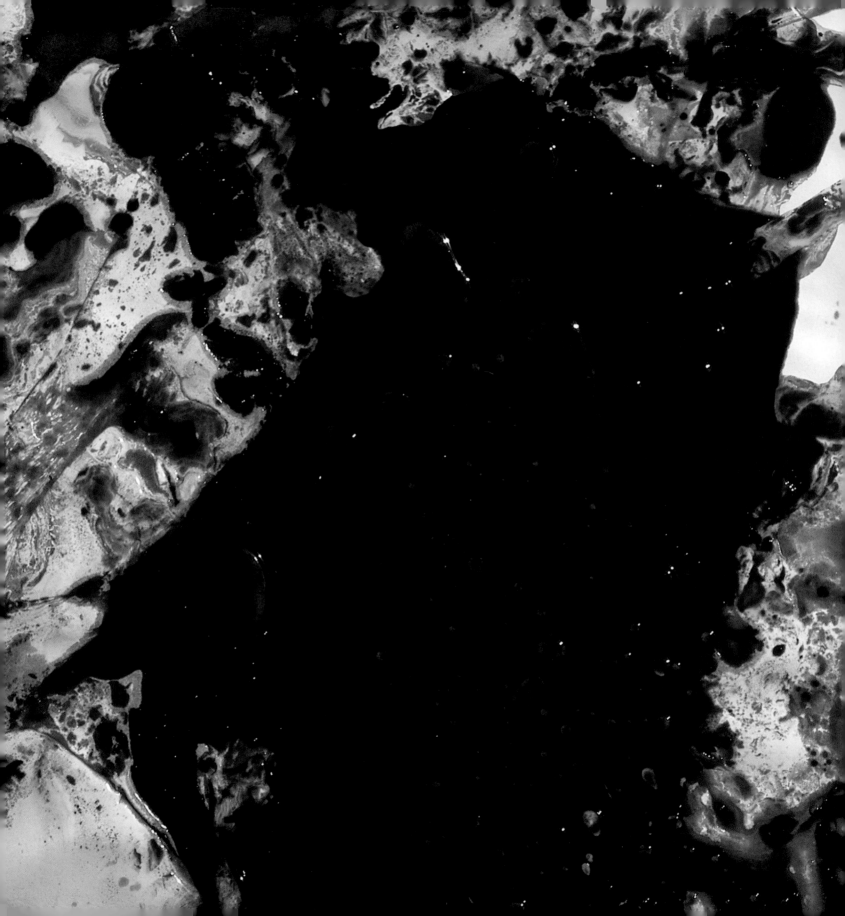

1. FLOTTA OIL TERMINAL Orkney Isles 1986–7

For thousands of years Flotta (or Flattey, the 'flat' isle of the Norsemen) slumbered, barely populated, at the gateway to Orkney's Scapa Flow. Three momentous events of the twentieth century were to intrude: a world war, rapidly followed by a second, put the island centre stage in Britain's naval strategy when it became the base for the Home Fleet; and, in the 1970s, oil arrived.

The first oil tanker was loaded at the newly-constructed oil terminal in 1977. Oil arrives at the Flotta terminal pumped ashore through a 30-inch diameter pipeline laid on the sea floor. The pipe is part of a system that gathers the products of the offshore oilfields Piper, Claymore, Scapa, Tartan, Petronella and Ivanhoe. At the terminal, impurities and salt water are removed and gases separated from the crude oil. Further processing of the gas produces high-value propane and ethane. These are exported as liquid petroleum gas by special tanker. The processed crude is stored in five half-million and two one-million barrel tanks from where it is exported by tanker to refineries in Europe and the United States.

Surplus methane gas is flared from the top of the 223-foot stack that can be seen from all around Orkney and the north coast of Scotland. The flare has become a symbol of modern Orkney in much the same way that The Old Man of Hoy has come to represent the natural heritage of the islands. Surplus gas is used to generate electrical power for the terminal and contributes to the national grid supplying Orkney with much of its off-peak needs.

Evidence of 5,000 years of civilisation is everywhere to be found in Orkney. Standing stones and burial chambers pre-dating the pyramids sit adjacent to the paraphernalia of the oilfield. Unlike the ancient beaker people, however, the oilmen have agreed to take their artefacts with them when they go.

The ecology and wildlife of the islands and surrounding seas are unique and very special.
The operation of the Flotta oil terminal has to be accomplished with the appropriate level of sensitivity to this natural environment.

Ronnie McDonald

Opposite Crude oil from Nigg terminal, on glass.
PHOTO: FIN MACRAE

August 1986

At Dyce I boarded the Occidental Orkney plane, a little red mail plane. The rest of the passengers appeared to be Oxy employees and their wives returning home from a shopping or business trip. The forty-minute flight was noisy and bumpy but the view was magnificent. Many thoughts and questions ran through my head as we landed. How would I react to working on site at this terminal, a place that I had avoided and tried to ignore on my previous trips when I was only interested in drawing the natural environment?

The next morning the taxi picked me up to drive me down to Houton Jetty where the Flotta ferry leaves for its eight-mile sea trip. On the way we were caught up in a cattle jam; a Hove farmer was moving his dairy cows. I was the last passenger to board, the boat was full and every one was wearing their blue parkas, the uniform of the Flotta worker. The atmosphere was very quiet. Phyllis Brown, the secretary for the administrations officer who was sitting next to me, introduced herself.

Right *Flotta* 1986
graphite and pastel

Above right
Big Colin.

Middle right
Tank farm, detail
1986
graphite and pastel

Below right *Tank farm,* detail 1986
graphite, pastel, pen and ink

After the twenty-minute boat crossing, vans and Land Rovers were waiting at the Flotta jetty to drive us up to the terminal, despite it being only a few minutes' walk. My first sight of this part of the island, which used to be the community's peat-cutting ground, was the outer building's security gates and the chalky sepia-coloured storage tanks, the tank farm: this was the visitor's introduction to the northerly terminal.

Phyllis checked me in at security and drove me up to base where I met Freddie, the administrations officer. We discussed my drawing schedule and security procedures. I noticed a pin-up calendar, the first of many I would spot on my various site visits. Phyllis gave me a tour of the terminal in the van: the tank farm, process plant, and terminal jetty and outer perimeter. There were hardly any workmen to be seen, only the sheep grazing on the raised landscape banks.

I felt both alienated and fascinated by this site. Here was a clinical, engineer-designed twentieth-century site placed in an area of wild, natural beauty. Whilst I was drawing, two workers, both called Colin, one an Orcadian and one from the north of England, offered to drive me around to find suitable locations to draw; they even brought along a chair for me. I concentrated on the forms of the tanks and the long line of pipes leading into the tank, and the spiral stairway that wrapped itself around the tank farm.

Above
The *Handa Lass* ferries workers to the terminal, day and night.

I was never left completely on my own. Workers came along in their vans to check I was all right. Two security officers, big burly men looking like brothers, walked along to speak to me; they knew some people from my home, the Black Isle. At the end of the day I was collected and taken down to the boat. Ian, one of the workers, offered to take me back and forth to the ferry for the week.

At breakfast in my Stromness B&B, I talked to Mr Brown, the owner of the guesthouse, who had done some contracting work at Flotta. He told me of the bitterness amongst some of Orkney's community towards the Flotta workers because of their noticeable affluence, new cars and houses. He also felt there was discrimination in having one boat for the contractors and another for the Occidental workers.

Out at the terminal, where I was drawing in the tank farm, there was a stillness and calm.

Over tea at base with the men, they discussed fishing and catching 'spooties', razor fish, on the shore. They spoke of how, when they started, their work was varied and demanding, but now their jobs were monotonous and less taxing. In recent years the company had cut back on its bonuses and luxuries. Seats on the air service to Aberdeen were now sought after. The catering budget had been cut but the meals were still free and coffee, tea, rolls and biscuits were available at all times throughout the terminal. The majority of the workforce was Orcadian and although they had complaints, they were thankful to have a job here.

Big Colin took me down to the terminal jetty where the gas and oil were pumped into tankers by LPGs, the loading arms which hang like giant operating arms of robots, black and menacing. A huge monster of an oil tanker was docked; when loaded the ship would head for Rotterdam with its crew of thirty Philippinos.

In the afternoon I was shown around the east side of the island where the gases, butane, ethane and propane, were separated from the crude oil and stored. Unlike the tank farm this area was fully exposed with multiple networks of pipes spread out all over. The smell of gases, the gushing hot steam and the deafening noise all hit me as Robert guided me under and over pipe passageways: numerous shiny stainless steel tanks and pipe lines glistened in the afternoon sunshine. It was eerie and I was very aware that this was potentially the most dangerous area of the terminal.

Fortunately for Orkney these oil operations are restricted to one site and a small island, and many island people have benefited from the employment in the past, bringing new blood to the area, 'Ferry Loopers'. A close watch is kept on this plant, however, for it is set in one of the most important marine locations, Scapa Flow.

On my return journey to this site I planned to look more closely at the island itself and at the people who live here and how they have been affected by this industry placed on their back doorstep.

Security Guards 1986
colour etching with chine collé

Knock Out Tank, detail 1986
pen and ink wash

Jetty 1987 pen and ink wash

Tugs 1987 pen and ink wash

August 1987

I checked in at the terminal hotel, the Hilton, located just outside the terminal's entrance. From my bedroom window I looked down onto the pier and beyond to the island of Hoy. Baby rabbits on the grass were enjoying the still warm evening.

The next morning I woke up early and strolled along the shore, seals accompanying me in the water. In the distance the *Handa Lass* was slicing its way through the calm waters of Scapa Flow bay, bringing day-shift and office workers. I made my way over to the office to greet Phyllis and was introduced to Bill Crichton, the administrations officer, who organised Big Colin to drive me to the terminal jetty where a Danish ship was loading ethane gas. Whilst I was drawing, some of the crew on board watched me through their binoculars from the control deck. In the mess at base I was made welcome by the men and I showed them my photographs and sketches from my previous visit.

In the afternoon I left the terminal's perimeter and walked up the main road of the island. This was my first time outside the base and I felt relaxed. In the terminal, because of the dangers and nature of the work, security is tight and my movements during the day were constantly monitored. Outside I was free.

One hundred and forty people live on smallholdings on the island. Looking eastwards, small crofts formed a long line of grassy fields down to the water line. I passed Helen's father, who was checking his lambs. Helen works at the base and lives with her parents; she also helps on the croft. I turned and looked back at the strange juxtaposed imagery of industry and crofting.

When dark fell, I returned to base, collected my security pass and made my way down to the jetty where a Japanese tanker was being loaded with oil.

The tide was out and it towered over the jetty. As I set up my camera with a fine-grained film and experimented with long shutter speeds, my only guidance in the dark came from the floodlights from the terminal and the ship. It was surreal to be walking in a deserted base with the gas flare's eternal flame burning brightly high up in the black skies. Occasional cries from the resident sheep and wading birds could be made out over the whistling cross wind. After midnight I made my way back to the hotel.

In the morning I took photos of the day-shift workers arriving at the pier. Later I made my way to the island's shop and post office run by Phyllis's parents, the Sinclairs, on their croft.

Mrs Sinclair welcomed me into their home. A woman of stocky, strong build, her small blue-grey eyes shone from a friendly, open face. The bank clerk and his assistant from Kirkwall were having their tea; they travel all over the islands offering banking services. Mrs Sinclair collected her shop keys and we walked to the shop, a converted croft house. The interior was typical of a small traditional island shop; it sold everything from groceries to rubber boots. After digging tatties for their lunch Mrs Sinclair invited me in for a cup of tea. Mr Sinclair was sitting on the rug in front of the hearth stoking up the peat fire. They talked about the construction years on the island whilst I tucked into Mrs Sinclair's delicious home baking.

A thousand men lived in the camps during the terminal's construction and the Sinclairs had been very busy with the post office and supplying clothing. The locals were invited to the centre dances with cheap drinks on sale at the temporary pub. They knew Dave Mackay from the Black Isle, a well-known character called 'The Hangman' for his approval of the death penalty.

Robbie, Flotta 1987 colour etching with chine collé

The combination of industry and crofting is a striking feature of the Flotta landscape.

He was a tall, strongly built man with jet-black hair who worked for a time on the construction site before working at Sullom Voe. His mother, Sarah, helped my mother in our house and made the best lentil soup. Dave had come to the Sinclair's door one day wanting a replacement for his broken work belt, but Mrs Sinclair did not have any 54-inch-waist belts in stock. He went away with a rope around his waist! Dave was still remembered for his singing at concerts and the Sinclairs had a recording of his famous rendition of 'North to Alaska'.

I returned to base in the evening and set up my camera using an infrared film in the darkness. I worked until the cold set into my toes and fingers and I returned to the hotel after 11pm.

The next day was very windy and cold. Luckily Bill offered me one of the terminal's vans to draw in and drive around. I parked the van looking down onto the tank farm with Scapa Flow and the main island in the background.

Sketch 1987 pen and ink wash with graphite

2/2   Eday III   Smith '84

Orkney Landscape I 1984 colour etching

Mrs Sinclair 1987 mixed media on paper

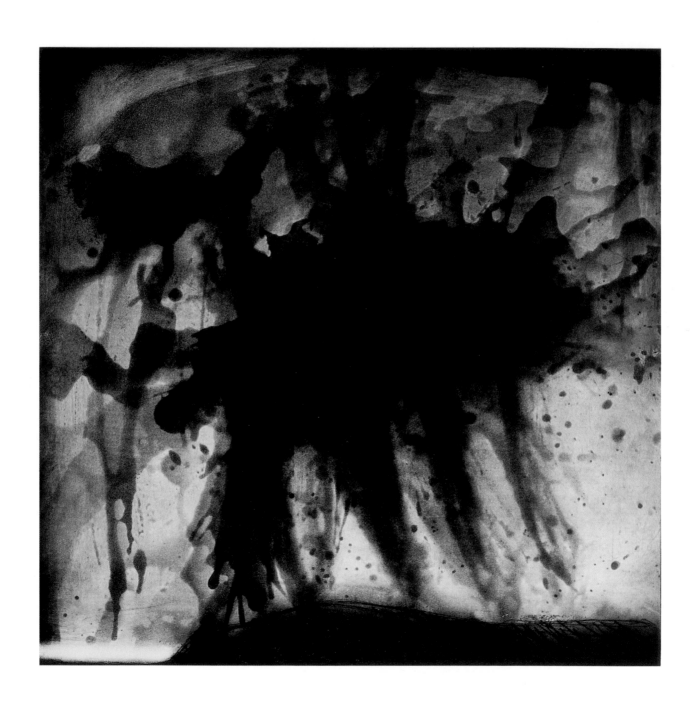

Orkney Landscape II 1984 colour etching

At lunch John Leggat, the Marine Superintendent, kindly offered me the chance to go out in one of the tugs in the bay to observe the two crude-oil loading points, SPMs, in the bay. I was driven down to the jetty and boarded the little green tug *Hoy Lass*. The weather had cleared up and the wind had died down. It was great to be out in a boat again. The skipper reminded me of a Spanish sailor: big brown eyes, shiny black hair and wearing a small gold anchor earring. He told me he and his wife travelled all over the place to country and western concerts: I could picture him in his cowboy outfit. An oil tanker was taking its load from an SPM. Looking like a large buoy coated in thick rubber, the SPM's huge long rubber-protected hoses ran up to the ship.

On the final day I took my usual early walk along the shore, where numerous seals basked on the sand in the morning sun. In the bay, divers were preparing to repair one of the damaged SPMs, which had been hit by a tanker the previous day.

I displayed my work in the office for the workers to see but unfortunately there had been a mix-up of times and I had to pack everything up and dash to the pier to catch the boat, luggage spilling out everywhere. I boarded the P&O ferry to Scrabster – another calm crossing – and sat out on deck reflecting on the week's visit and appreciating the opportunity to stay on the island. I now had first-hand experience with which to compare the island's way of life to the terminal's daily operations.

Flotta Jetty 1987 pen and ink wash

From REMEMBERING MAGNUS

The sea is above us
The sea will defeat us
The sea will cover us
The sea is hungry
The sea is my pillow
The sea suffers no escape
The sea is my armour

George Gunn, 2000

Orkney Landscape III 1984   colour etching

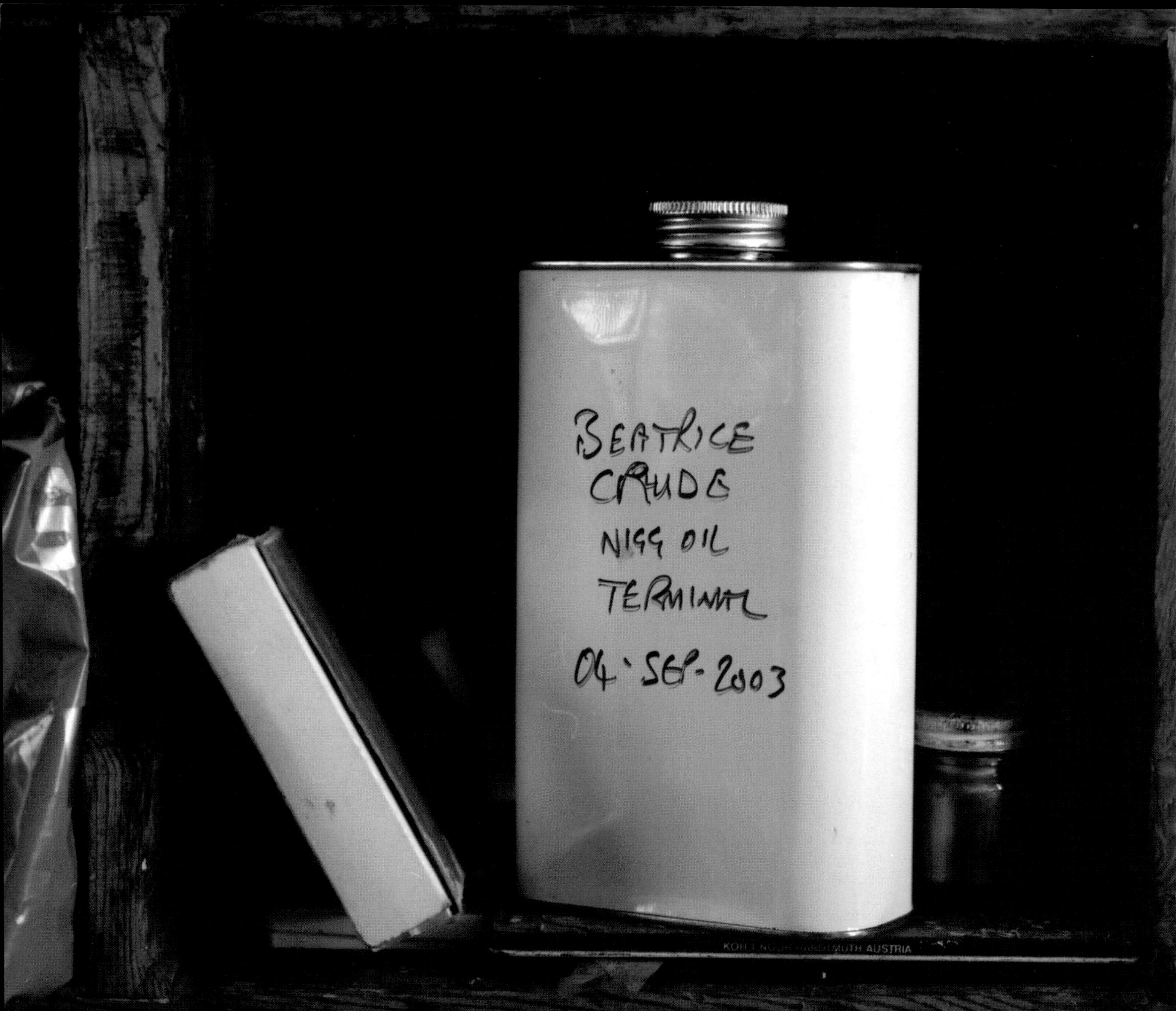
BEATRICE
CRUDE
NIGG OIL
TERMINAL
04 - SEP - 2003
AUSTRIA

2. NIGG CONSTRUCTION YARD Easter Ross 1986–7

'Cathedrals of steel' was a term often used to describe the great steel structures that emerged from Highlands Fabricators' Nigg yard on the Cromarty Firth in the 1970s and '80s. The intricate lattice works of high-tensile tubular steel were erected onshore and towed out into the North Sea. There they were fixed to the sea floor with giant steel piles driven deep into the bedrock below to support the oil production platforms that made Britain a world-class oil producer for thirty years.

Man's intrusion into nature's order on the north shore of the Cromarty Firth was abrupt, a consequence of urgent economic necessity. The first to arrive were the Americans, steel workers from Louisiana who had direct experience of this kind of construction work. Thousands of travelling men from all parts of the United Kingdom were soon present, living in every available B&B within a fifty-mile radius. By 1974, a camp adjacent to the yard and a redundant Greek cruise liner berthed alongside housed thousands more. Boom time. Over a period of years the company training school trained local men and women as steel fabricators and the itinerant workforce gradually dispersed.

The yard's fortunes have ebbed and flowed with the price of a barrel of oil. The North Sea oilfield is commercially viable only when the oil price is relatively high. Consequently, periods with empty order books were frequently experienced. Nevertheless, the yard did evolve over time and offered a range of skills and facilities capable of delivering an operationally complete oilrig.

As the North Sea oilfield continues to mature and the big fields decline, the yard's management and workforce have striven to diversify into non-oil related work. The hope is that the yard can survive in some form to ensure that oil's legacy to the people of the Cromarty Firth is work and prosperity and not yet another derelict site.

Ronnie McDonald

Opposite
Artist's studio 2005.
PHOTO: FIN MACRAE

August 1986

I set out from my home in Munlochy for a forty-mile scenic drive over the Black Isle and Easter Ross. Driving through Alness and Invergordon I could see the Highland Fabricators' construction yard in the distance, its huge cranes and workshop hangars set against the backdrop of Souter's Cliff.

Nigg Bay was once a quiet, pink, sandy shore where local families picnicked and bathed. It was now engulfed by Britoil's oil terminal for the Beatrice Field and by Highland Fabricators. Anchored in the Cromarty Firth were eleven oil rigs in for service or waiting for work, just like the naval fleet in the First and Second World Wars.

Childhood memories flooded through my head: protests from local people against industry coming to the Cromarty Firth in the form of aluminium smelter; family outings standing with the crowds on the Souter watching the launch of Nigg's latest completed order; Nigg shift workers in the village waiting for Kenny Smokie, Newton's bus driver, to pick them up for work; tales told of workers losing their entire wage packets gambling in the bus on their way home; heavy drinking sessions in the village pubs; and fast flashy cars on the roads.

In the head office I met up with public relations manager Bill Shannon, a small, friendly, bearded Glaswegian and an ex-journalist. Over coffee he told me some stories of the yard's heyday in the 1970s when money and labour were plentiful. The company recruited willing candidates regardless of their references and the company paid expenses on top of their wages. No records were kept of the thousands of men employed. Bill had a company car, free petrol and other perks.

Above *Boys of the North* 1986 mixed media on paper
Left Rig being towed between the Cromarty Sutors in 1986.

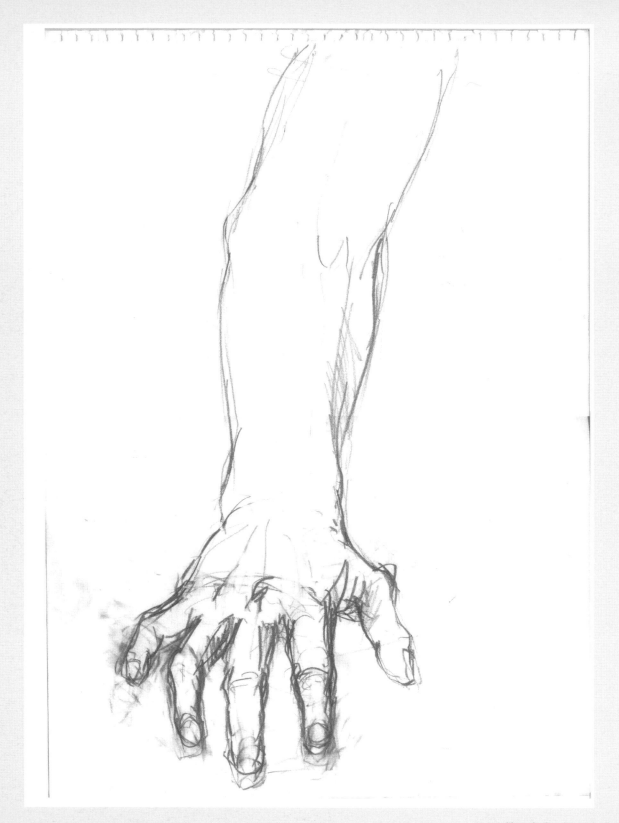

Sketch for *Lorrie's Catch* 1988 graphite

Things had changed. Orders were fiercely sought as the demand in oil fabrication had fallen. Nigg had recently lost an order due to an industrial dispute over the introduction of refurbishment work on rigs and platforms. The workforce was unhappy with the company's changed working conditions: men on differing pay rates working alongside each other, longer hours and for less pay. In the company's eyes the union's terms were not cost-effective. Nigg was well known for its strong union, its workers being known as 'Darkies of the North'. They were thought to have been strongly influenced by the socialist-minded Clyde workers who moved up to the north.

Before taking me on tour around the yard in one of the company cars, Bill briefed me on safety regulations on site: he handed me earplugs, a safety hat, glasses and boots. The yard itself was a vast expanse of industrial landscape with five main workshops and a huge dry dock: provision for welding, painting, rolling steel and construction. Outside were battered and graffitied old portacabins, neat piles of machinery, and discarded sections of cranes. Scraps of unwanted metal lay all around, remnants of the yard's previous twelve years of work.

Bill left me and I returned to shops one and two to start sketching and take photos of the industrial scene in front of me: the immense scale of the building and rig constructions; the acid olive-coloured light beaming down from the spotlights high above, hitting the orange steel structures below; the deafening echo of grinders, welding works and hydraulic lifts; the pungent smell of smoke with bright orange sparks flying from the welding torches; the hundreds of men working inside, outside, on top of and underneath the massive and still growing orange structure, the air cold, damp and unwelcoming.

Right Former workers at Nigg construction site had left their marks for others.

The Nigg workshops were on a massive scale
and seeing them for the first time was almost overwhelming.

Shop One 1988 mixed media on paper

Shop Two 1988 mixed media on paper

One of the Nigg store huts where the men collected tools and materials for each day's work.

Work took place inside the shops as well as outside in the open air.

As I walked around, men stopped their work, raised their welding helmets and stared down at me. News spread through the shop that a female visitor was present and being constantly monitored by hundreds of curious eyes made me feel rather uneasy. But I would have to get used to the working conditions if I were to continue drawing in these environments. I tried to find a sheltered spot away from swirling drafts. There were so many images to reflect upon: enormous cylindrical volumes of steel veiled in complex, irregular shapes, ladders and hundreds of wires and leads. Amongst all of this I began to recognise familiar faces from Munlochy and the Black Isle: Willie Gardiner, an ex-farm worker at Belmaduthie and now a foreman, Allan Oman and one of the Ross brothers.

Part of the construction was being lifted over to the other end of the shop by the huge hydraulic crane, so I walked over to shop four where a module for Shell was under construction. As I climbed up the ladders and along the scaffolding, the scene before me resembled a science fiction fantasy, a labyrinth of complex machinery and computer rooms.

At noon the lunchtime siren sounded. Men appeared out of their warrens, scuttled down ladders and marched hurriedly out of the shop towards the canteen huts. I had never seen such a mass of workmen, of all shapes and sizes, all of them wearing their brightly coloured welding caps. Only the foremen and the inspectors remained to check the morning's work, and a still silence settled over the shop. Once the workers returned from their break, I packed up my equipment; the cold was penetrating, and I made a note to put on my warm clothes for the next visit.

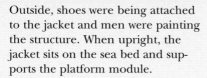

Outside, shoes were being attached to the jacket and men were painting the structure. When upright, the jacket sits on the sea bed and supports the platform module.

Bill Shannon told me that there was going to be a big lift this morning – one of the four shoes was being locked into position on the jacket (these shoes, placed at the jacket's base, sit on the sea bed). A giant crane hoisted the shoe up slowly; it would take several hours to position it. Smaller cranes circled around, lifting men up in metal buckets. Suspended and swinging in the air, they engineered the manoeuvre from intercom radios. Tiny figures of men were standing at the top of the jacket getting a good view of this growing ominous giant.

Later on, a workman took me up to the top of the jacket in a wire cage. The weather, though rather windy and bitter, was sunny. There were few people around as the yard was running a four-day week. Long, narrow scaffolding walkways were built on top of the giant steel legs to serve as gangways. As I stepped on to the top of the structure the wind blasted in my face but the view was panoramic: I could understand why the visiting Irish priest had said to Bill Shannon, 'This is the nearest I will get to God.' Welding generators, leads littered everywhere, men welding under protective plastic sheeting in all corners and levels. As I looked down I could see men, seemingly fearless of heights, climbing up steel ladders attached to the legs of the steel structure. I spoke with Allan MacDonald, a welder from Balintore. Dressed in a thick suede jacket, gloves and leggings, with a thick navy canvas hood covering his head and shoulders, he looked more like a warrior archer than a welder. He was pessimistic about the yard's future.

Over a coffee in the offices, Bill seemed depressed. He was uncertain of any new orders being won; there was a staff of 300 but a workforce of only 200. The life expectancy of the yard had been ten years but it was still going after fifteen years.

The jacket's temporary walkway for workers and
sketches of the cranes working on the jacket construction.

Above The arrival of oil affected the economy and landscape of the entire Cromarty Firth.
Below *Tree of Gold, Milnafua* 1988 graphite and gold pigment

Many 'industrial nomads' have settled in the north, saving money, buying homes, finding other jobs in the area when laid off. Shilling Hill was the first estate built to cater for the industrial boom. Coul Park, Ferryhill and Westford followed. Some estates were affluent, but not Cadwell Wood Caravan Park and the adjacent Milnafuah estate, north of Alness. The caravan park had served as temporary accommodation for Nigg workers (even ships had been used for a time in the 1970s). A decade later it sadly catered for those evicted from council houses and other homeless people. Abandoned and wrecked caravans lay askew amongst silver birch trees. The terraced wooden houses of Milnafuah still stood but their walls were covered in graffiti, and they were surrounded by disused old cars, some burnt-out.

I talked to Rab Wilson, a shop steward from the Amalgamated Union of Engineering Workers (AUEW) construction section and a long-time joint union convener at Nigg. Having cut his teeth in the Edinburgh building trades, he arrived at Nigg in 1972 where he had remained ever since, bar a brief period of redundancy in 1988.

Sometime cynic, sometime eternal optimist, Rab was a canny conversationalist: 'In a sense the company needs the unions, often to act as a secondary police force, telling the men what they can and cannot have according to the agreement.' As he rose from his desk in the union portacabin after an hour-long conversation he shrugged and remarked, 'Ah well, as Marx said, nothing to lose but our chains.'

Above right *Niggers of the North* 1988 pastel and graphite
Below *Sketches*, Nigg 1988 graphite

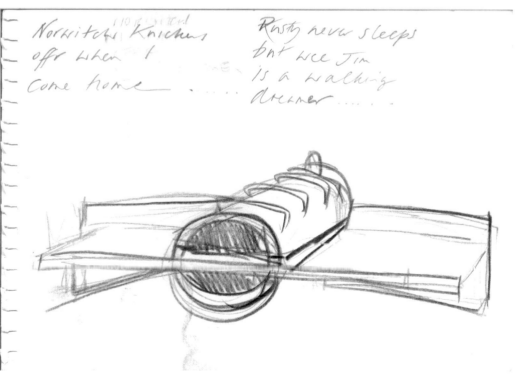

Norwitch's Knickers
off when I
come home . . . . .

Rusty never sleeps
but wee Jim
is a walking
dreamer . . . . .

Shop Two 1988 pen and ink wash

CONSTRUCTION SITE

In its own swamp
a clanking beast, painted like a toy,
guzzles a ton of muck, then, stretching up thin,
turns its head in disgust to spew
its horrible mouthful out, raining it down
in a battered truck that lurches towards the dump.

High overhead
a little insect, constructed like a man,
crawls on a foot-wide thread on a web that catches
only a space with a cloud in it. A crane
staggers, peeps over, drops its long neck and clutches
in tiny mandibles a steel straw from the ground.

The cloud goes by.
The space is patient, lending itself to be
new forms, new spaces. Growing like crystals in
a depth of space, they order it and say
ascending fits in the chaos between
the grovelling beast and the pecking crane in the sky.

Norman MacCaig, 1966

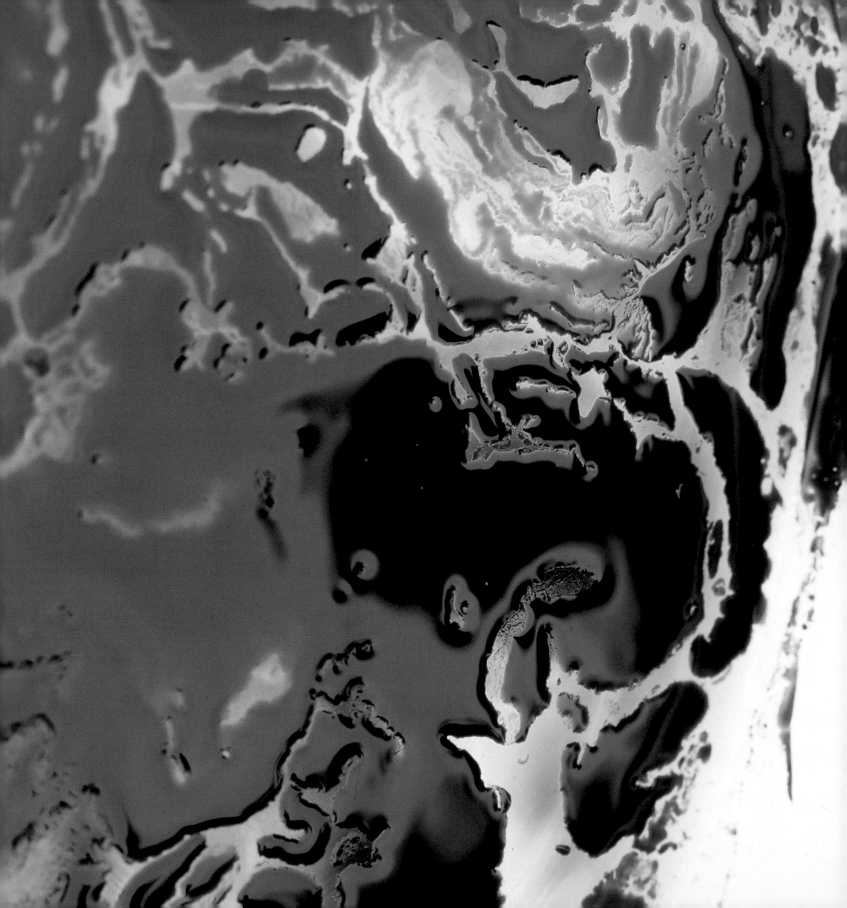

All the superlatives of the day were used to convey the scale of what went on at the Howard Doris Loch Kishorn construction site in the mid-1970s. The biggest hole ever dug in Europe, it was said to be second in the world only to the Kimberly diamond mine in Africa. Its purpose was to construct the Ninian Central oil production platform for Chevron. After four frenetic years of activity the platform departed for its North Sea destination, described as the largest man-made object ever to move across the face of the Earth. At 400,000 dead weight tonnes, it certainly took some moving. For statistical completeness, mention must also be made of the prodigious volumes of stout and lager consumed by the itinerant workforce over those years. In the camp on the remote north shore of the loch, and on redundant cruise liners moored alongside, 3,000 men and women worked hard, and played much the same way.

The importance of the Ninian Central project to the UK economy in the mid-1970s cannot be overstated. A series of energy crises and OPEC-sponsored crude oil price hikes had put many western economies in a precarious state. The prize for the United Kingdom of getting the Ninian Central on stream on time was nothing less than oil self-sufficiency for the nation. It was to be the central gathering point for oil and gas from numerous oilfields in the North Sea. From Ninian the oil is pumped ashore to the Sullom Voe terminal in the Shetland Islands and the gas by another pipeline to the Scottish mainland.

Loch Kishorn had been chosen as the construction site because a number of fortunate geological accidents made it ideal. Firstly, the loch was sufficiently deep to take the draft of what was to become the largest floating structure built to date. Secondly, aggregate and ballast of the precise type essential to mix the one-third of a million tonnes of concrete necessary for the project was available from a local quarry.

Loch Kishorn has reverted to serenity. The facility did not develop into the centre of heavy industry in the Western Highlands and Islands that some had hoped it would (others are equally relieved). The camp and fabrication sheds have been levelled, the ground landscaped to hide the scars, the workforce dispersed and, except for the great hole blasted from the rock on the loch's northern shore, nothing remains.

Ronnie McDonald

Opposite
Crude oil from Nigg
terminal, on glass.
PHOTO: FIN MACRAE

Tea Time at Kishorn 1986 colour etching with chine collé

November 1986

The skies started to clear as I drove into Lochcarron, or Jeantown as it was once known. The winding road narrowed over the hill from where I got my first sight of the yard; Santa Fe 140 oilrig was anchored in the water waiting for its next offshore assignment. I had seen this rig in 1984 in the North Sea when I was on board the Stirling Teal cargo vessel, my first offshore trip and the genesis of my 'Oil Worker Scotland' imagery.

Sheep roamed the green park outside the perimeter where once rows of workmen's caravans had been parked. At the entrance the yard's battered sign-post stood with nearly all its paint peeled off. I reported to the security office and then drove along a pot-holed track to the other end of the yard where the head office was located.

Above Britain's highest public road over Bealach nam Bo.
Below Loch Kishorn construction yard from Jeantown.

trout
salmo trutta

Salmon Trout 1987 colour pastel on paper

The men were known as the 'Kishorn Commandos'.

I was greeted by Kirsty Murray, secretary to David Burgess, the public relations manager. Kirsty, from Lochcarron, was the first woman to be employed in the yard, in 1974. David informed me that the yard was in receivership but was allowed to finish off its last order, two modules for Total. Moving work to Nigg and Ardersier would be too costly.

When the yard had first started operating, work was plentiful: men turned up at the main gate from all over the country and were immediately taken on the company's payroll. Special buses and trains ran from Inverness for the workforce and there was a workers' boat service from Skye. David was understandably doubtful of the yard's future; as yet no company had expressed an interest in taking it over. Although sad about the closure, David had the security of his own business: two pubs, one in Dingwall and the other in Inverness.

A young, shy man with kind blue eyes, nicknamed Danny 'The Pet', showed me around the yard. Originally from the south of Scotland, he and his wife and children now lived in Lochcarron.

Worker, Total Module 1986 mixed media on paper

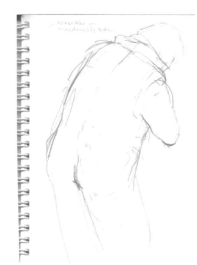

Above Abandoned portacabins were everywhere on site.

Below Sketches 1986 graphite

We drove to where the modules were under construction, both roofed over with corrugated iron and polythene for protection against the wintry conditions. They would soon be moved onto barges ready to be towed away. We climbed up the scaffolding steps and onto the modules. It was very dark undercover, spotlights replacing the already disappearing dim winter's daylight. Men were working at all levels and at all angles, fearless scaffolders balancing on steel poles. People stopped to chat, pose for photographs and make raunchy suggestions: Geordies, Lancashire men, Cockneys, Glaswegians and Irish all shouting out. Suddenly the tea-break siren sounded and men emerged from dark corners and holes. These men were what were known as the 'Kishorn Commandos'.

During the tea-break I walked down to the jetty while the men sat in their huts near the barges. One particular Cockney worker seemed to pop up everywhere while I was sketching the modules under construction. Eventually, he stuck his head out from one of the huts, inviting me in for a cup of tea, an offer I declined. This cheeky charmer seemed innocuous enough but the local reputation of the Kishorn workforce as 'the scum of Europe' had gone before him. Many of the 3,000 who had once worked at Kishorn had lived in an accommodation camp. No women were permitted inside. Instead, prostitutes regularly hung about outside the gates waiting for custom. The camp was now deserted, littered with empty, gutted portacabins tipped onto their sides. The still-operating 'wellie bar' was the workmen's main source of entertainment in the camp. Over the years it had witnessed many a night of heavy drinking, some regularly spending £30 night after night. The company owned the bar, and its wage packets were frequently returned through the till. That night I popped my head into the bar: a solitary figure stood feeding coins into a fruit machine.

Tangle 1987 pen and ink

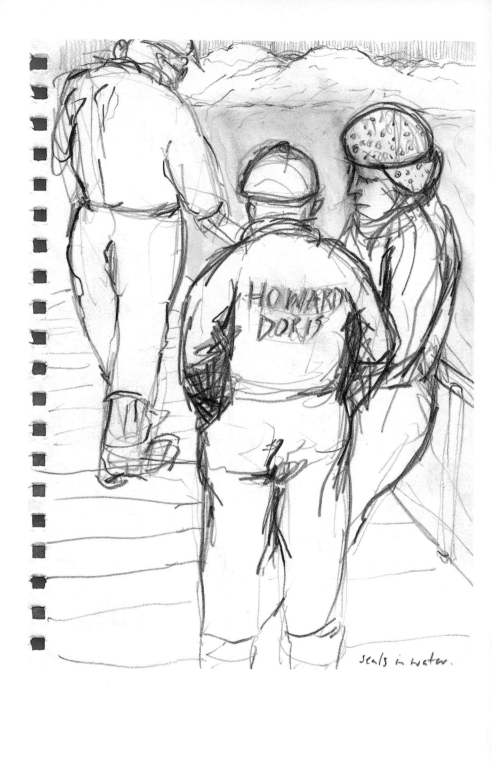

Sketches 1986 Waiting for tea-time and watching seals in the water

In the warehouse a fat, bearded Irishman was clearing up. He told me that he was seeking construction work on the Channel Tunnel or at Sizewell nuclear power station. Here was a latter-day version of the nineteenth-century navvy, always on the move wherever work could be found. Many others were trying for jobs on the same sites. As the rain began to lash down I sheltered in the warehouse with Danny 'The Pet'. He told me of his plans to emigrate to Australia where his brother-in-law was. He looked forward to an improved, more secure life.

On the ground outside, exposed to the loch's punishing breezes, I gazed up at the high pass Bealach nam Bo flanked by the hills of Sgurr a'Chaorachain Meall Gorm. This is one of Britain's highest public roads, rising to a height of 2000 feet above sea level. At the old dockside I peered down into the vast, deep, black water-hole, man's own creation. I reflected on the time of the building of the dock, a huge operation to gouge out this colossal great hole from the hill's rock face. This dock had been the embryo and cradle for the creation of what had been at the time the world's biggest-ever concrete structure. That gigantic jacket had been built for the deep North Sea waters of the Ninian Field, off Shetland's north coast. Now the enormous floodgates remained shut. David Burgess had informed me that it cost £30,000 to open and shut these gates.

Above the door of the tea hut hung the plaster cast of a man's head impaled on a pole. Splashed in paint an inscription read: 'When will the Mohican return?' When I asked the men in the hut the significance of this cryptic message, they all chuckled and told me it referred to an infamous character from Nairn who wore a wig wrapped around his head like a turban.

Above Sgurr a'Chaorachain Meall Gorm.
Below Paint store.

The workforce often picked out anyone displaying eccentricities in appearance or manner; the victim would be endlessly teased.

Everyone was fair game. Photographer Craig Mackay, then a welder at Nigg, told me a famous tale. When a visiting VIP guest was escorted around the site, one of the workers' favourite tricks was to lean down from an upper scaffolding deck and attach a greased polystyrene cup on each side of the guest's hard hat. Whilst the workforce were in stitches, the escorting site managers were too embarrassed to inform the innocent victim that he was walking around wearing a Mickey Mouse hat.

Another legendary tale from this construction yard was that of the 'Strawberry Jam Kid'. Someone was going around squashing strawberry jam sachets into plans and drawings around the yard and everyone was getting extremely irritated. One evening, a superintendent was in the 'wellie boot' bar, ranting and raving, 'If I get my f…… hands on him, I'll f….. kill him'. He turned around to pick up his pint and there was a strawberry jam sachet at the bottom of his glass.

In the evening Julie, the assistant to the manager, whose house I was staying in, invited me to the hotel pub. Hers was one of a complex of company houses built in Strathcarron. There was to be a farewell party for a friend of hers who had an interesting and well-publicised private life: married and maintaining two girlfriends, with girlfriend number one jealous not of the wife but of girlfriend number two. We were joined by two other Kishorn workers. Alastair, a short fair-haired Yorkshire man with glasses and a bulging beer belly, was as ever bemoaning the fact that he was short of money, even though he was one of Tarmac's

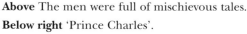

Above The men were full of mischievous tales.
Below right 'Prince Charles'.

top engineers, on £60,000 a year. His friend was a quiet and sober man from the suburbs of London. Whilst Alistair got increasingly drunk, his companion sipped a soft drink and snacked on unsalted crisps.

The time had come to pay my final respects to the dying yard so I walked around as the morning sun melted the overnight frost beneath my feet. An English guy, nicknamed 'Prince Charles', stopped to talk to me. Soon to be made redundant, he was thankful that he had his croft. He lived in Applecross and was married to a girl from there. I recognised a Geordie worker heading for the 'wellie bar'. His unshaven face and blood-shot eyes betrayed a night spent drowning bitter sadness at the news of his redundancy.

MOLADH NA LUINGE

Chluinnte faram aig an fhairg'
molach garbh anns an aisith –
beucach, rangach, torrach, searbh,
srannach, anabharrach, brais i.

Coinneach MacCoinnich, c. 1792

THE PRAISE OF THE SHIP

You'd hear the noise of the ocean,
rough and shaggy in contention –
roaring, wrinkled, heaped and bitter,
it was snorting, riotous and brash

Kenneth MacKenzie

St Fergus 1991 mixed media on paper

4. BP FORTIES FIELD North Sea 1986–7

When BP's drilling rig Sea Quest struck oil 170 kilometres off the Aberdeen coast in 1970 few at the time realised the full implications of the discovery. Within the space of a year, appraisal drilling had revealed a huge oil reservoir covering an area of 91 square kilometres and containing over three billion barrels of valuable light crude oil. The discovery was named Forties: the UK's first major oilfield.

In the autumn of 1975 the first oil to be pumped ashore from the North Sea's UK sector brought the Forties field on stream at the rate of half-a-million barrels a day, equivalent to one-quarter of the UK's daily oil requirement.

The development plan for Forties was a pioneering engineering feat. Nothing like it had been done before in the North Sea. Four identical fixed steel production platforms were installed, two of which, Charlie and Delta, were constructed at Highland Fabricators Nigg Bay yard on the Cromarty Firth. The platforms were positioned in the summers of 1974 and 1975 and a fifth platform, the Forties Echo, constructed by Highland Fabricators, was added in 1986.

The productive life of the Forties field was initially estimated at around thirty-five years. However, recently developed enhanced recovery techniques are expected to extend the life of the field up to fifty years. A feature common to many old established oilfields is that smaller adjacent reservoirs of oil, not in themselves economically viable, can now be brought on stream economically by linking them back to established infrastructure such as the Forties.

Crude oil, natural gas and condensate are pumped ashore from the Forties through a 36-inch pipeline laid on the sea floor. After landfall at Cruden Bay in Aberdeenshire, the oil is transported through a buried 36-inch landline to the BP refinery at Grangemouth in Central Scotland. There, fuel oil, petrol and feedstock for the chemical and plastics industries together with fertiliser and a host of other products are manufactured from the Forties high-grade hydrocarbons. Crude oil, surplus to Grangemouth requirements, is loaded onto tankers berthed in the Firth of Forth and exported to world markets.

Ronnie McDonald

Opposite
Detail of crude oil
souvenir from
BP Forties.
PHOTO: FIN MACRAE

Rob at his Desk 1987 mixed media on paper

November 1986

On the way from Aberdeen railway station to BP headquarters at Dyce, the taxi driver told me the shocking news of the Chinook helicopter which had crashed off the Shetland coast en route from Brent Shell platform to Sumburgh airport. There were only two survivors.

At BP Headquarters I met John Pack and Judi Meek, the public affairs team who were to accompany me on the trip. I was shown two films, one based on their exploration in the North Sea and the other on BP's Forties Field, which I was to visit. They were interesting films but very one-sided in their oil propaganda message. Afterwards I was taken to the Holiday Inn close by, which had the added attraction of an adjacent cocktail bar where, over a pint, one could watch swimmers in the pool nearby. I was entertained by Judi at dinner, all part of BP's VIP treatment.

Next morning I rose at 6 am and after breakfast Judi and I drove to the heliport where I was helped into a survival suit. These are made of thick rubber in a bright red/orange colour and everyone travelling in a helicopter must wear one, hopefully saving its wearer in the treacherously cold North Sea waters should the helicopter crash.

On the drive out to the helicopter I sat in the back seat with two men, one of whom was still tipsy from the previous night's entertainment at Mr. G's nightclub in Inverness.

Alcohol is not allowed offshore so he had brought it with him still running in his blood. His breath smelt of old fermented whisky. He was an electrician and had moved around a lot in his working life, once working at Nigg.

We boarded the helicopter and everyone put on their ear protectors or earplugs and fastened their seat belts. The whole craft shuddered with the vibrations from the take-off and the conditions inside were very cramped. All the men were absorbed in copies of *The Sun* or *Daily Record*, reading of the previous day's Chinook disaster. Between patches of fog I could see the waters of the grey-green North Sea. The chap beside me indicated that we were about to land on the safety vessel.

The sea wind blasted my face as I was escorted down the steel steps to the indoor waiting room. Suddenly it struck me that I was offshore, hundreds of miles from dry land. For me this was an utterly strange, unknown and all-male territory. I asked if I could walk around outside whilst we waited for our next helicopter and a man named Chris Hayman escorted me.

Outside we looked over to the recently installed Forties Echo platform, which was as yet unmanned. It looked like a dated spaceship. The safety vessel we were on was a floating installation and it was listing from side to side from the strong current and the force of the sea below.

BP heliport 1987.

" Platforms and rigs eat men's souls. Half your life is spent away from home; you have two lives in one."

Offshore worker

Off to work, BP Forties 1986.

Left Forties field from Forties Bravo platform.

Right Men leaving for shore.

Back inside, I sat next to a man who looked no older than twenty-one. He was waiting to go onto a platform for the two-week shift. Dark-haired, with a thick moustache, his arms and hands decorated in tattoos, he had the appearance of a gypsy. Back in Liverpool he had left behind a young wife and three children. He didn't enjoy his job but he had a growing family to support. Eventually it was our turn to go up onto the helipad. Our helicopter was very small and glass-fronted and we had excellent vision. The pilot circled around all four platforms, which stood like strange metal creatures emerging from the sea, bellowing fire from their flare booms.

As we came in to land on Forties Bravo platform, the drilling tower, cranes and decks looked immense crammed onto the installation. But the heli-deck space itself was incredibly cramped; over its edge lay the sea hundreds of feet below. Down in the office quarters, Ian Robertson, the installation manager, introduced us

to Ron, a big, burly Yorkshire man and the platform's chief fire officer who came in to act as guide for the day. He showed us first the deck of our lifeboat in the event of an emergency evacuation. No camera flash was allowed, as it would trigger a reaction from the UV flame detectors, which in turn activate the fire protection water deluge system. The very lowest level of the platform was deemed too dangerous as the wild waves crashed against the legs and well conductors.

The sea was all about us as we walked along the stairways, which hung over the side of the platform, the cold, blustery day magnifying the power of the threatening sea. The vast emptiness created an eerie timelessness. For Ron, systems like the Christmas Trees (the valves on the wellhead through which the oil arrives on the platform from the reservoir below) and turbine engines are simply part of an everyday process pumping oil to onshore.

Waiting for the Call I 1987 mixed media on paper

Fisherman I 1991 conté and charcoal

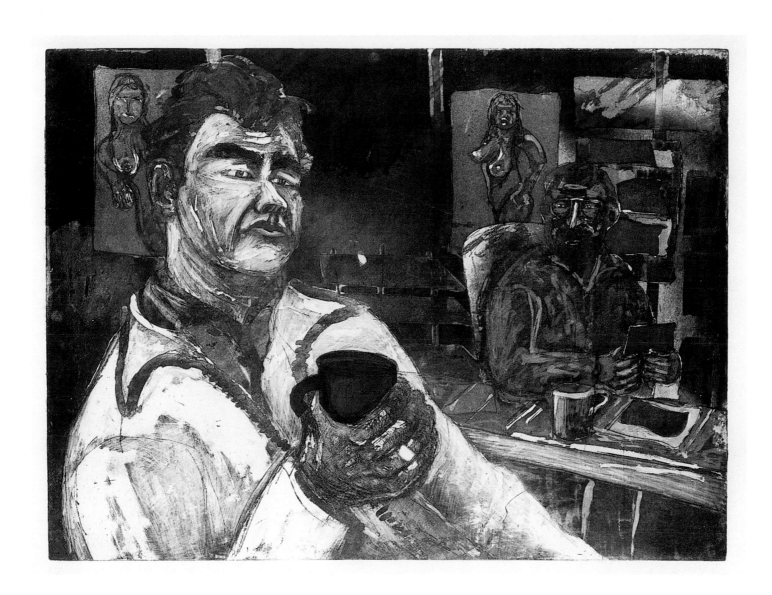

Tea Time Offshore 1987 colour etching with chine collé

Forties Bravo Platform 1986.

For me, however, some of the machines resembled mysterious passageways and the bowels of some strange, huge monster. The living quarters were soundproof and all boots had to be taken off once indoors. But I could still smell oil and chemicals wafting in from outside. The inside was a glorified portacabin. In the canteen the catering contractors had made an attempt to brighten the space with red checked tablecloths and by providing a false cottage window scene hung on the wall.

Our return flight was delayed for an hour by the weather. On the homeward journey my head was full of so many images that it would be difficult to know where to start when I got back in the studio. I would have loved to have stayed longer to draw more.

Untitled sketch 1986 graphite

Afterword, July 1987

I felt it was important to give the BP Forties offshore workforce an opportunity to see the series of visual work I created after my visit. In the main, these were people very unlikely to visit an art gallery and with little or no knowledge of contemporary art.

My initial idea was to hang my etchings and mixed media paintings in the canteen and recreation area out on BP Forties Field. BP, however, vetoed the idea of an exhibition offshore but agreed to a display of my Forties Bravo work at Dyce heliport. The waiting lounge there is a depressing room with garish red plastic vinyl chairs arranged in four long lines back to back, with two large television screens at either end of the room blasting forth twenty-four hours a day. For many of the thousand men who passed through the lounge while the display was on, it was an unexpected shock to see images, portrayals of themselves in this way. Disappointingly, but not surprisingly, BP did not purchase any of the pieces; they were not glorifications but harsh reality based on the workers I saw. Grampian presenter John Duncanson did a small radio piece interviewing the men on their reactions to the exhibition.

Tree sketch 1989 graphite

Waiting for the Call II 1987 colour etching with chine collé

THE DERRICKMAN

Bird of the monkey board
pulling out of the hole
eyes like chipped marbles
wrapped up in a hanky

never eat, stomach tight against belt
tied to the derrick like a buoy
to pull stand after stand
until the hair on the head swims

and breakfast flies through the air
like an exploded grouse
and the only glory a raxed back
and the elastic arms of a sad gorilla

a human machine part
of blood and rope
a sentry of muscles
on the way to the sky

and through the gate of the seabed
we were digging, digging
into the formation where the thing
that will finally hold us is waiting

George Gunn, 1978

Opposite *Detail from Rough Sea I* 1985 etching

When peace came in 1945 the creation of a sustainable industrial base and high levels of employment in the Highlands and Islands of Scotland became a vision cherished by successive governments. The pre-war public works programmes had provided foundations on which to proceed. The construction of hydroelectric schemes across the Highlands had reached a zenith in the inter-war years and, to this day, the schemes are an enduring success story accounting for some 20 per cent of Scotland's off-peak electricity capacity.

State-fostered technology in the 1960s brought us Concorde, Dounreay and advanced gas-cooled reactors. In the Highlands of Scotland it brought aluminium smelting and paper pulp manufacturing on a global scale. Locally available natural resources, hydroelectricity and forestry, were utilised and seemed to justify the expenditure required. Oil's arrival in the early 1970s at first gave additional impetus to this programme of economic regeneration.

Onto the scene in 1972 arrived the prominent American construction outfit, J Ray McDermott Inc., to set up the Ardersier rig construction yard just east of Inverness. The yard was one of seven similar facilities opened by various international consortia throughout Scotland around this time. Again, local resources were the key. Cheap (make that mostly free) land adjacent to deep-water channels facilitated the construction and launch of large structures. Important too was the availability of a willing workforce, not to mention substantial state aid to assist in the purchase of plant and equipment.

So, how fares the economic renaissance thirty years on? Papermaking, pulp manufacture and aluminium smelting all ceased in the 1980s and '90s. The Ardersier rig construction yard too has closed its gates despite the international market for offshore oil platforms remaining buoyant. Three decades of excellence were unable to sustain the yard. Switching the lights off as he left, a company spokesman said: 'Bidding for global fabrication is not a viable option [for Ardersier] as the company is well placed to cater to our customers' global demands through its facilities in other parts of the world'.

Ronnie McDonald

Opposite
Crude oil from Nigg
terminal, on glass.
PHOTO: FIN MACRAE

November/December 1986

I set off from Munlochy in the winter's dim morning light, a forty-minute drive in the car. Nearing the site I could see the yard's high cranes towering above the Ardersier forestry plantation. Turning down onto the long straight road, as wide as an aeroplane runway, leading to its entrance, the yard came into full view. Built on a once- flat sandy shore, its vast workshop hangars and huge jacket surrounded by cranes dominated the shoreline with its rural and scenic panoramic backdrop. In their heyday Nigg and Ardersier had provided full employment for the local workforce and although in competition with each other they would work well together in terms of swapping workforce if one yard was busier than the other and in need of certain skills. Times had changed however. There were fewer orders and therefore less work available.

At the gate I reported to security, one of a series of makeshift office portacabins at the entrance. Tom Sneddon, the safety officer, a small, stocky middle-aged ex-paratrooper, showed me around. He handed me a hardhat, boots and safety harness in case I slipped at the top of the jacket. We drove in his van along a waterlogged track that was deep in mud in many places as it was used so often by the heavy industrial machinery.

Left Ardersier from the Black Isle.

Above, clockwise Ardersier diary entry, the safety officer and the site manager.

Left
The jacket
on its side.

At the end of the track lay the jacket on its side, a huge metal titan in the making. At its base we stared up at the men working high above, poised at all levels at precarious angles on this steel giant. We climbed the wide scaffolding stairway, which zigzagged its way to the top. It was very windy and the plastic covering sheets were flapping wildly but the view was magnificent looking down onto the sandy banks and tidal Moray Firth waters.

I was glad to get back on the ground where we visited one of the huge open draughty hangars where two modules were being assembled and where most of the men were working.

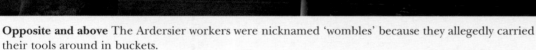

Opposite and above The Ardersier workers were nicknamed 'wombles' because they allegedly carried their tools around in buckets.

As I walked among the welders I came across one character, George McDonough, who doubled as a photographer in Nairn. He gladly stood and posed by the welding generators. There was no real shelter for the men working on any part of this site even in the huge shops. Afterwards I walked around the perimeter of the yard. It was lunchtime and most of the men had disappeared to their tea huts, but one welder was sitting outside on a slab of concrete having his flask of tea and piece. His backdrop was the water across to Eithie and Cromarty Souters on the Black Isle. Few industrial workers could claim such a splendid lunchtime view.

Some months before I had clambered all along the coast from Eithie to Cromarty Souters accompanied by Ben my Labrador in order to gain a better viewpoint of this yard from the Black Isle side.

Dipping down steep marshy gullies and walking along the edges of the fields avoiding the sheer cliff faces below, I could hear the workings going on across the water, the echoing, banging sounds of industrial activity. I had tried to draw this imposing view whilst Ben disappeared into the broom and whins chasing after rabbits; the site itself had looked very vulnerable and exposed to the open mouth of the Moray Firth and out of place in the surrounding natural beauty.

Below *Three sketches* pen and graphite
Right The artist's father tending his hives on the Cromarty Sutors in 1987.

In the distance tugs had been towing an oilrig destined for anchorage in the Cromarty Firth. I had not stopped to look for any fossils on Eithie shoreline as I walked towards the Souter to get a closer look at the rig as it was tugged past between the narrow necks of the land gateways. My father had been waiting there at the Souter for me to help him lift his bees onto the pick-up and transport them off to Scatwell, for the heather.

Walking around the yard now was an eerie experience. This windy, desolate, dusty industrial acreage seemed without atmosphere or character. It was quite unlike the other yards I had visited. It had no sense of identity; it was soulless, purpose-built. It may seem strange to talk of oil yards having individual characteristics but I felt the lack of them here strongly. It brought to mind the very transient quality of the gold rush experience in the north as compared to Fort George barracks built by the English in the mid-eighteenth century to quell the rise of the Highlanders after Culloden, and still in use today by the British Army.

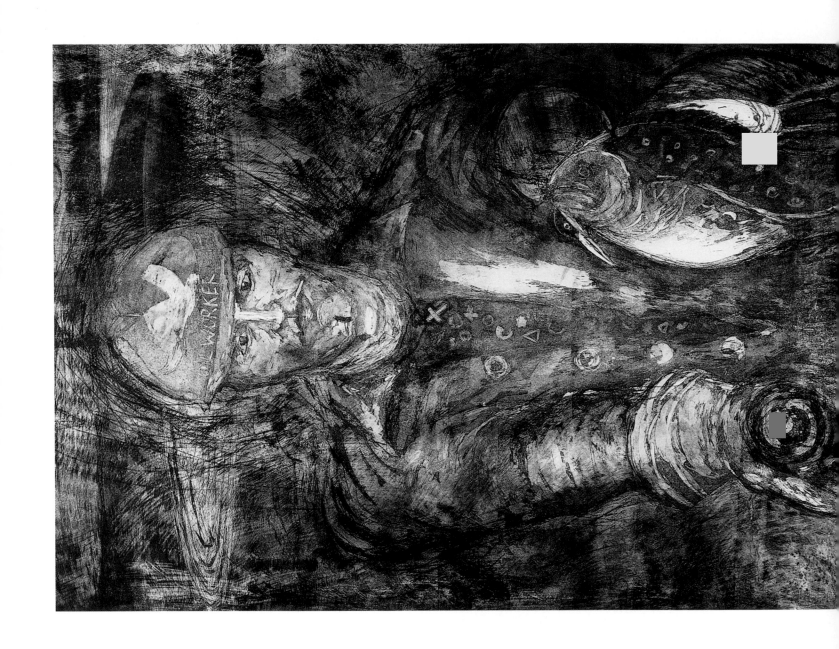

Oilworker 1989 colour etching

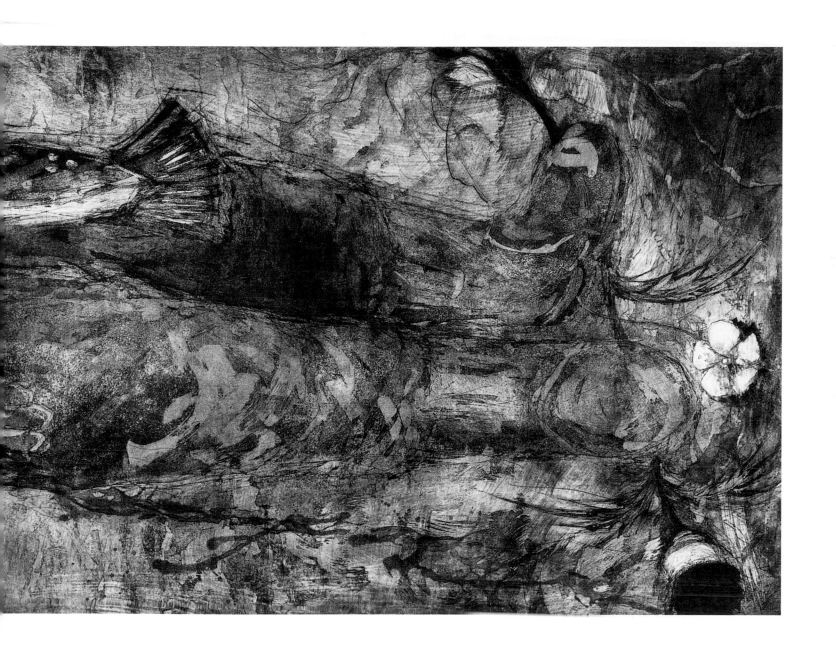

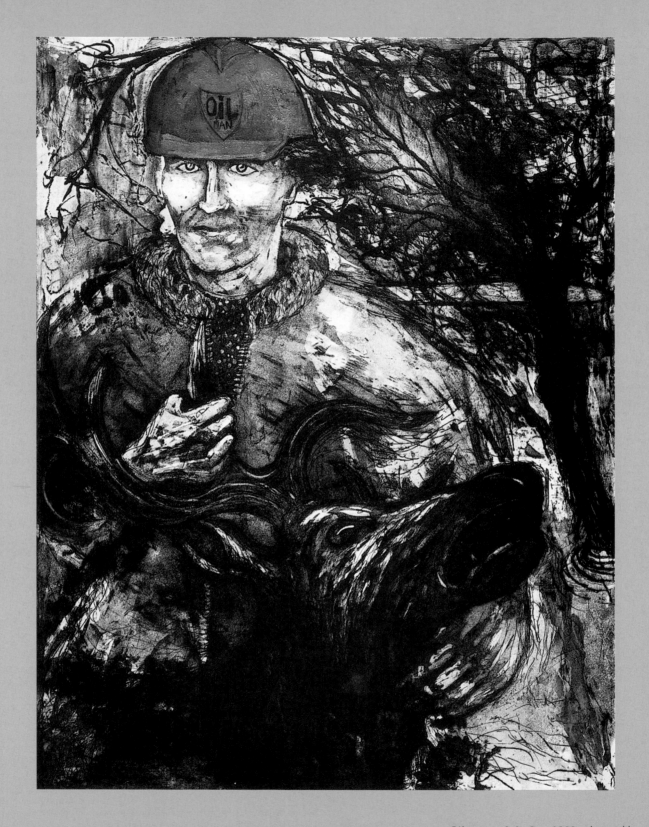

Oilman and the Stag 1989 colour etching with chine collé

CAUL KAIL

Rigs stan erect, great iron teats
on the briest o the sea.
We sook the black milk up and up
until the wall gangs dry.

And gin the ile's aa teem and deen,
The bonny fish aa catchit,
Fit then? Tartan toorist whigmaleeries?
Trips roun the roosty ile-rigs?

Ken Morrice, 1979

6. ARNISH CONSTRUCTION YARD Isle of Lewis 1986

In 1974 the Norwegian shipping and construction conglomerate, Fred Olsen, established the oil fabrication yard at Arnish Point on the Isle of Lewis. Local people thought it a tremendous opportunity for major economic and social regeneration. The creation of work opportunities at home had the potential to reverse a century of emigration; Lewis's young had little choice but to look to mainland Scotland and beyond for work and a future.

Periodically, over twenty-five years, the yard did provide prosperity for some and reversed, albeit temporarily, the island's population decline. At its peak in the early 1980s nearly 2,000 men and women were employed fabricating a wide range of structures and modules for the North Sea oilfields. The island economy benefited from injections of people and cash but, overall, the venture's full potential was never quite realised. The cyclical nature of oilfield construction contracts led to ever-longer periods of lay-off and, in 1983, the yard closed and Fred Olsen moved on.

Shortly afterwards, the facility was acquired by the Dutch construction firm, Heerema. It reopened amid great expectations following the discovery of oil in significant quantities in the westerly approaches of the Atlantic Ocean. Again, the sporadic nature of oil-related construction work made itself felt and, in 1990, a management buy-out brought the facility into local ownership. Lewis Offshore Ltd completed an offshore loading turret for use on one of the new Atlantic oil fields and in 1998 the yard once again closed its doors.

For generations people have been a main export of the Western Isles and of Lewis in particular. A glance at virtually any phone book in any town in Canada, Australia or New Zealand will confirm this with names such as MacLeod, Morrison and MacIver. Not just farmers, but mariners too have made their mark. In the 250 years that Britain was the premier maritime power, more ship's masters per head of population came out of the Isle of Lewis than from any other community in the Empire. The Arnish yard will be remembered as the cause of the return of many natives.

Ronnie McDonald

Opposite
Artist's Studio 2005.
PHOTO: FIN MACRAE

December 1986

As we disembarked at Stornoway, a cutting sharp wind and a carpet of frost on the ground was the winter's greeting from this harsh, flat, peaty land. I took a taxi to Lewis Offshore Yard at Arnish Point just outside Stornoway. Daylight was just beginning but there was no sign of the winter's sun. The road leading to the yard was narrow and winding, and black-faced sheep waddled, unconcerned, across our pathway.

The driver dropped me off at the head office and I struggled in with my luggage, portfolio, camera case, tripod and materials. Mary Ann MacKenzie, assistant to the yard manager, Colin MacDonald, welcomed me and introduced me to the other staff, mostly all islanders. Martin, a shy, young yard worker, walked me down to the yard past the security shed and through two big iron gates. Compared to the northern-based yards, Lewis was small in scale with a workforce of only 400.

By the water's edge barges were being built for Marathon, the welders working under plastic tents well protected from the bitter elements. In the welding shops a module and a small jacket for BP were under construction, part of the four-legged jacket stood outside; the familiar industrial smells and noises hovered all around. I started to draw and take photos of the welders working on the barges. To the west across the Minch I could make out the snow-covered hills of the mainland.

At lunchtime the girls invited me to Zebo's in town, a trendy island bar with continuous 'disco inferno' music. Looking out of the bar window I could see some of the moored fishing boats. This town is one of the most important fishing ports in Scotland.

In the afternoon I drew inside the yard's construction shop, out of the bitter winds. Most of the men stopped to talk to me. I was used to these disruptions by now.

Left Arnish yard.
This page *Sketches* 1986 graphite

Opposite and above
Two studies, *Arnish yard welding shop* 1986 graphite with pen and ink wash

Detail from *Carmina Gadelica exhibition*, 1997 sandblasted glass

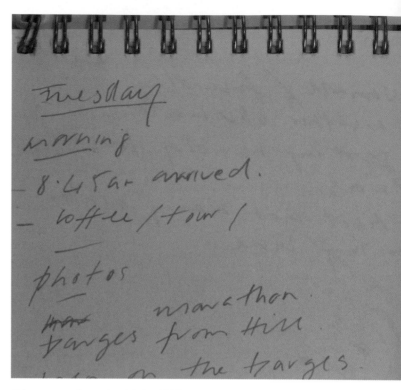

Diary entry from Arnish in 1986.

Talking to people who worked in these locations was important in building up a complete picture.

In the evening we went to the Caberfeidh hotel for an evening drink. Mary Ann talked about her move to Lewis. Although her parents were born-and-bred Lewis folk, she had been brought up in Glasgow. The isles and the Gaelic were close to her heart and she loved living here. She dropped me off at the Hebridean guesthouse where I was staying, which was run by a hospitable English couple. The three boarders, all workers at the yard, were having their supper. Later we all walked down to the Crown bar. Around the table we discussed island life. The three men were from the south; as outsiders they found the islanders' strict Sunday Presbyterian practices somewhat difficult. Everything was closed.

The Free Church still maintains the strongest, and still-growing, congregation in this area. The minister preaches in spartan surroundings; there is no interior ornamentation. In many parishes a precentor leads the singing of the psalms, which are sung in Gaelic without organ accompaniment. The voices are reminiscent of ancient droning whaling sounds. There is a word in Gaelic which describes a person who finds the faith: *coorum*. My mind wandered from our conversation to the image of my great-grandfather's bible, *An Tiomnadh*, finger-marked with constant past use, now lying untouched in the cupboard shelf at my parents' home. Drinking is a huge problem on the islands and we would witness this in the bar that evening before the Sunday curfew.

John, Welder at Arnish 1988 acrylic on board

Fishing and oil provided employment for islanders.

Fisherman II 1991 conté and charcoal

I got up early on Monday; it was dark and frosty. I put on numerous layers of protective clothing and set myself up for drawing, sitting on my donkey chair in the midst of all the hammering and construction. Under the acid orange light I could hear some of the men shouting over to each other in Gaelic, their voices hardly audible against the noise from the welding, grinders and overhead crane trundling along with its heavy loads.

Giant sheets of steel were being unloaded from a ship. I walked over to draw and take photos. The men all turned around, smiled and waved. One of them, John MacDonald, a minister's son and crofter from Lochs, looked more like an ancient Celt than a welder. Dressed in his welding balaclava and protective gear, his piercing blue eyes and strong facial features stood out against the backdrop of the wild Minch waters and the treeless windswept land. The frost started to gnaw at my fingers and toes whilst I was sitting drawing, so I retreated indoors.

Above John MacDonald.

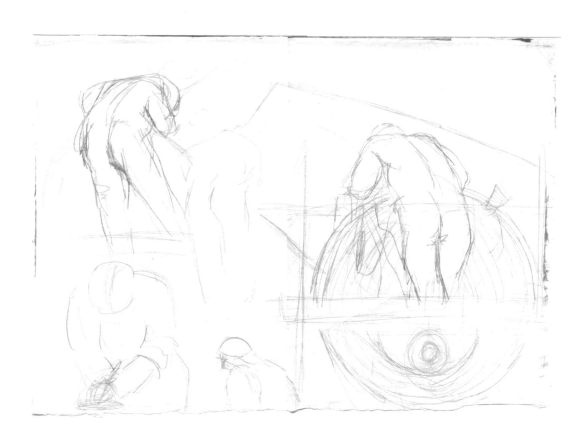

Sketches 1991 graphite and ink

Sketch, Arnish 1986 pen and ink wash

Islander 1988 mixed media on paper

In the afternoon I visited 'Kenny the Nose', the storekeeper. He was sitting by his bench reading the *West Highland Free Press* with the local Gaelic radio station on in the background. In his slow and soft melodic island accent he announced that I could come in for a cup of tea anytime: 'The kettle is always on the boil.' We sat around the electric fire sipping our tea, putting the world to rights. Occasionally a workman would come to the hatch and ask for some equipment needed for his job.

It was my last day. The sleet blasted into my face like small stinging needles as I waited for Mary Ann to collect me early in the morning. This was the eve of Heerema's Christmas dinner dance and Mary had brought along two of her stylish outfits for me to choose from to wear for the dance.

In the yard a double shift was working to clear up before the fortnight's break. I met John, who was staying at the guesthouse. He showed me around his department – the paint workshop. Here the men spray at high-pressure tiny particles of carborandum onto the pipes to clean them before applying protective coatings of paint. The smell of paint fumes hung heavy in the air, irritating the throat; I was always advised by the men in the yards not to go near this area. John shone a spotlight onto a worker to enable me to take a photo. Out from the dim light a painter wearing his hood and dust mask looked up, his blue eyes shining against the light like a frightened animal caught by surprise. I was glad to walk out into the light and fresh air again.

I returned to the stores for a cup of tea. Angus and his pal were playing crib. I started to draw them. Angus became embarrassed as he noticed the pin-up calendar behind me and was about to turn it around. I said I was used to seeing these calendars hanging around the yards. Kenny walked in, complaining of his cold feet – an occupational hazard of working in the stores. We both crouched around the two-bar heater and he and Angus talked about their children, who all spoke Gaelic. It was important to them to hand down the language to the next generation.

Above 'Kenny the Nose'.
Below Unknown masked painter.

The yard's last day of work before the Christmas break in 1986.

At noon I walked down to the security gates where the guards were preparing for the big Christmas hand-out: a choice of a turkey or a bottle of Famous Grouse whisky. I could see the men starting to walk over. I set my camera to capture the long line of bright orange jackets, blue jeans and rigger boots coming towards me. A queue formed as men stamped their feet in an attempt to keep warm, their breath frozen in the air. Walking past me they grinned and raised their bottles aloft before hurrying over to their cars and speeding off up the hill to home and preparations for the evening's festivities. John from Lochs shouted over to ask if I was going to the dance.

In the evening I met up with some of the girls at the Caberfeidh Hotel. Looking around one could hardly recognise the men, now clean-shaven and smartly dressed in their best suits. Soon after the meal the dance started up and I could hardly keep my balance in my precarious pink high heels dancing reels. The drink flowed and conversations were in full swing when suddenly the hall drew silent as a woman started to sing a Gaelic solo lament. The dance disbanded by 'auld lang syne'. John drove me home via the Carlton bar; he had to dip his sheep the next morning. I suspected he needed to dip his own head too.

From BETWEEN SEA AND MOOR

On summer days how innocent it [the sea] looks, how
playful, how almost Mediterranean. How easily like a
human being it is transformed from serenity to anger,
from calm to sudden outbursts of rage. On an island
the sea is always present. Always one hears the sound
of it behind the painted day, a background, a resonance,
the loved and feared one.

Iain Crichton Smith , 1979

North Sea 2004 PHOTO: ROBERT POGSON

7. PIPER ALPHA PLATFORM North Sea 1987

Situated 110 miles off Aberdeen, the Piper oilfield was discovered in 1973. Covering some 12 square miles, the reservoir produces oil, gas and condensate. Condensate is a valuable, but very volatile, mixture of liquid petroleum gases indispensable in the manufacture of petrochemical feedstock for the chemicals and plastics industries. Piper Alpha was connected to other platforms and to the shore by a system of four pipelines laid on the sea floor, one for oil and three for gas. Oil was exported ashore to the Flotta terminal at Scapa Flow in the Orkney Islands. Gas was received from the nearby Tartan platform, mixed with Piper's own, and pumped to the St Fergus gas terminal north of Aberdeen. Piper Alpha also exported gas to its sister platform, Claymore, situated 21 miles to the west.

On the evening of 6 July 1988 the Piper Alpha was destroyed by fire and explosion. Of the 226 persons on board, 165 perished together with two crewmen from the MV Sandhaven who died in a heroic rescue attempt. Major refurbishment work on the platform's hydrocarbons processing systems was being undertaken. Nevertheless, the decision had been made not to interrupt production. Operators on the night shift attempted to activate equipment that had been partially decommissioned during the day shift, thereby causing hydrocarbons to leak and ignite. As the fire spread the pipeline risers containing high-pressure gas and condensate ruptured. The resulting inferno destroyed the platform. Sixty-one men escaped and were rescued from the sea.

At the subsequent public inquiry the senior Scottish judge, Lord Cullen, declared that management of the platform had been grossly deficient. The judge did not confine his inquiry to the events on Piper Alpha. The general manner in which the offshore oil and gas industry was regulated and managed was scrutinised by the inquiry. Cullen's recommendations led to a root-and-branch restructure of the safety regime offshore. His intention was to ensure that such a disaster could never again occur.

The operator of the Piper Alpha on the night of the tragedy, Occidental Petroleum, sold up in 1991 to Elf Enterprise. The new replacement platform Piper Bravo came onstream in 1993 and is now operated by Talisman Energy.

Ronnie McDonald

Opposite
Piper Alpha
Helideck 1987
infrared

Tony the Chef 1988 mixed media on paper

Dozing on the outward flight to Piper Alpha platform.

Extracts
from the
artist's
diary:

July /August 1987

The helicopter flight from Dyce was an hour and a half of constant vibration and noise. I tried to draw some of the men sitting in their seats in rows with their bright orange suits and earphones, reading, sleeping or staring into space.

On arrival the Offshore Installations Manager, Colin Seaton, a Yorkshire man, greeted me. I took off my suit and was led down a flight of stairs to my cabin, which was situated beside Colin's office.

The medic, Gareth Watkinson, took me to lunch in the large canteen where Trisha, the only other woman on my flight out, joined us; she was on a day visit. She was in charge of statistics for safety standards and this was her first time offshore. Accidents offshore are

very frequent but this platform had recently managed to achieve a hundred days without any. After lunch Colin introduced me to Jack Patience, the head safety officer, who gave me a run-down on emergency procedures and showed me the life raft which I would need to go to in an emergency. Colin gave me a tour of the platform outside but in my trainers I found it difficult to keep my grip. The metal grid walkways were very slippery due to the wet weather. Colin showed me around the well heads, oil and gas separation, gas compression and power generation in order to familiarise me with the lay-out. We returned to the office and Jack phoned Aberdeen to ask for a pair of rigger boots to be sent for me on the next flight.

Untitled 1988 mixed media on paper

Bond Shop Man 1988 conté and charcoal

Whilst waiting I chatted to some of the men inside. The bond shop opened up, a tiny shop selling duty-free perfumes, aftershave, cigarettes and sweets. In the dispatch area the men were waiting for their delayed flight and I asked what they thought of having women working offshore beside them. Most did not like the idea; it was a man's domain and most of the jobs were not suitable for women.

Trisha said goodbye as she went out on deck to board the helicopter back to Aberdeen. At supper, Tony, the chef from Shipley in West Yorkshire, teased me about being trapped with over 160 men for some days. Gareth came in with my boots, which had arrived with the flight. I was so pleased that I could start to work outside.

The film *84 Charing Cross Road* was being shown in the cinema, but few of the men were interested in watching it. There were no porn films on show when I was around but the men told me they were frequently shown and popular. I walked outside for a while trying to come to terms with the fact that I was offshore and familiarising myself with this alien environment.

I retired to my cabin at 10.30 pm. It was very quiet. The day shift were either sleeping or resting. As I lay in my bunk bed I could feel the vibrations of the turbines and generators, their muffled noises pulsing through our sound-proofed and pressurised cabins. The smells of oil and chemicals wafted and lingered in the air.

My cabin was designed to hold two men, with bunk beds and a shower/toilet. It was very cramped but more comfortable than cargo vessels. Many of the platforms constructed for North Sea operations are first and second generation and accommodation is very tight.

Piper Alpha flare 1987 infrared

In Norwegian waters, where they employ many women in such fields as engineering and geology, the accommodation and the working conditions are significantly better: their working schedules and hours are different and they have different labour laws.

The men on the rigs have to be very tolerant of each other as they live and work for two to three weeks in cramped, stressful conditions. Many are ex-servicemen who are used to a tough isolated lifestyle. The majority of those working on the platform are employed through a sub-contractor. There is no real job security and the contract is renewable every one to two years.

Top Supply vessel deck 1987 infrared

Middle Boarding the helicopter.

Bottom Supply vessel from the platform.

The day shift starts at 7 am and by 8 am the canteen was deserted. I walked outside to find the supply boat standing off near the platform below, with the pedestal crane unloading its cargo on to the platform. The boat seemed so small bobbing up and down on the sea. Looking down on the vessel it reminded me of my first trip offshore in the Stirling Teal. I remembered looking up from the ship's deck in very rough December seas at the massive structure of the Montrose Field with its gigantic crane lifting off its cargo.

Gareth offered to take me down to the 40-foot deck; the 20-foot was dangerous as the sea was very rough and waves were lapping over. At the 40-foot level I was near the well conductors – huge round long rods which bring up the oil. Another helicopter was coming in so I dashed up to take a few shots of men disembarking and boarding in lines of bright orange survival suits and soft travelling bags. Nearby, a series of scaffolding levels were being erected, the men outstretched and overhanging the platform with nothing but the sea below.

Before supper I had a quick game of table tennis with Gareth in the games room. The view from the window was of the drilling deck and gas flare. It was a lovely clear evening; on the sea below a supply vessel was delivering its cargo and in the background the safety ship was making its eternal circle around the platform. Every platform has a safety vessel. The work must be arduous in its monotony; three solid weeks being tossed about on the sea.

On deck I talked to John Wakefield, an electrician from Grimsby. His father was a fisherman but he did not want to follow that tradition. He was bored with the work on the rigs but the money was good and he had family commitments to maintain. He told me incidents of SAS men carrying out invasion exercises up the platform: men scurrying around in combat gear climbing up its legs and taking over control in forty seconds. Crane driver Derek Hill from Forfar signalled me to come and operate the crane. I helped unload a small package containing cigarettes ordered from the ship's crew. Sitting in the driver's cabin gave me a splendid view, the sea being directly beneath.

I rested until 10.30 pm, then went outside to walk around and take some infrared shots on the deserted platform levels. It was a dry but windy night and my only companions were the noises of the platform machines as I walked up onto the deserted heli-deck. Looking around from this vantage point I could make out the neon lights of the sister platforms belonging to Occidental, Tartan and Claymore. The lights on the deck illuminated the words Piper A and looking out into the blackness I could see the delicate flickering lights of the safety vessel on the pitch-black sea. I angled my camera down into the deep dark pit which was the sea, the noise of the waves lashing against the well conductors. It was like a strange timeless dream with the acid lights shining onto the metal against the forces of the sea; no one would hear my cries if I fell overboard.

The next day Gareth gave me a tour of the operating and control room where each well is monitored and controlled. One man became highly embarrassed and apologized to me for his use of strong language. But I had come to witness men working in their normal relaxed ways. The room itself was taken up by rows of monitors and computers; most of the computers were rather dated but new ones had recently been installed. The men told me that the platform was ageing and cracks in its legs had to be repaired every summer by divers. We visited Eddie, one of the engineers, in his work hut in the middle of the generator room. It was impossible to communicate as the noise was piercing, the smells pungent and unhealthy. To me his job constituted a health risk as he wore no ear protectors.

Whilst walking back to reception Gareth told me how he drew the strength to continue with his job from his Christian faith, strength he needed to deal with the working accidents onboard, especially at the drilling deck. During lunch a man sitting next to me warned me jokingly not to come in to eat when the 'bears' were eating: they eat all their courses on the same plate at one time.

On my way to draw out on deck I passed Gareth, Tony and Jack chatting. They were talking about women working offshore. Jack said that his wife would leave him if women were allowed on board and a guy from the pool table room shouted over that he would have to wash and shave regularly and mind his language.

Outside I sat and tried to draw some of the most striking details of the platform; the wind was in the right direction for the gas boom to provide constant central heating. I watched a seal tease a seagull with a fish in its mouth on the sea below; it would leave it floating on the water and just as the seagull was about to dive, it would grab it. Close by I noticed an oil slick in the form of a thin slithery line like a snake.

Block and Tackles 1989
conté and charcoal

Piper Alpha Crane 1987
pen and ink wash with pastel

Rigger II 1988 Colour etching

John the Electrician 1988 mixed media on paper

> "When you go home it's not that you feel good, but that you are back to normal. When you arrive home you make love to your wife and then put your bag down."
>
> *Offshore worker*

Rough waters usually break these up but it was calm today. John, the electrician, told me that oil companies are allowed to discharge five barrels of crude oil per day, but in fact they discharge a lot more. Given that there are 123 oil platforms in the North Sea, the implications of what he said greatly depressed me. Helicopter pilots are asked to look out for oil slicks and report them but many go unnoticed. In the evening I spoke with Tom Morris. He told me that many accidents and happenings offshore never reach the public eye. The Tartan field is apparently six miles off its original location site. The man who miscalculated its placing shot himself. Tom told me he was bored with his job, the excitement of the industry had gone and he would prefer to work on a drilling rig. On a platform the routine is slow and there is little to do.

On the final day I got up at 7 am. A friendly shout of 'Hello sunshine' from Tony the chef was not echoed by my sleepy, lethargic body. I tried to finish off my drawing on deck until the rain really pelted down. I packed my bags and waited for our delayed flight. At last I said good-bye to the men I had got to know. When we touched down at Aberdeen I have never seen a group of men move so swiftly, wriggling out of their survival suits and tossing them aside before fleeing through customs and running out to taxis or awaiting minibuses. It was a picture of men being granted freedom.

Fhaoileag bheag thu,
fhaoileag mhar'thu,
Fhaoileag a shnamhas gach cala,
Thig a nall is innis naidheachd,
Cait an d'fhag thu na fir gheala?
Dh'fhag mi iad 'san eilean mhara,
Cul ri cul is iad gun anail,
Beul ri beul, a'sileach fala.
Gur e mise th'air mo sgaradh
Ma tha ur leabaidh anns an fheamainn,
Mas e na roin ur luchd faire,
Na reultan ard ur coinnlean geala
'S ur ceol fidhle gaoir na mara.

Little gull, gull of the sea,
gull that swims every harbour,
come over here and tell a story,
where have you left the finest men?
I left them in the island in the sea,
back to back and without breath,
mouth to mouth, dripping blood.
It is I who am heart-broken
if your bed is in the seaweed,
if the seals are your watchmen,
the high stars your white candles,
and your violin music the scream of the sea.

Anon.

8. UIE CONSTRUCTION YARD Clydebank 1987

An epoch ended when shipbuilding ceased at the old John Brown's Clydebank yard in 1972. Shortly afterwards the yard was reborn as an offshore oilrig construction yard. To make space for the fabrication and assembly of large offshore modules most of the large berth cranes were demolished. The historic slipways on which the *Lusitania, Aquitania, Queen Mary, Queen Elizabeth* and *QE2* as well as battleships from the *Hood* to the *Vanguard* were created were covered over. The new owners, Marathon, took over in 1972 from Upper Clyde Shipbuilders. UIE (UK) Ltd took over in 1980 and finally, Kvaerner, the Norwegian engineering group, used the yard until it was mothballed in 2001.

Notwithstanding the cyclical nature of the oil-related fabrication industry, the yard did have a very successful three decades constructing jack-up drilling units and modules for offshore oil production platforms. Module work was something the yard did particularly well. On an offshore oil production platform the various functions such as power generation, hydrocarbon processing, crew living quarters etc. are often installed offshore in virtually complete form called modules. In the early years of the industry much of this work was done *in situ* offshore. However, the cost of maintaining a large construction workforce offshore became prohibitive. UIE was able to supply modules from the yard in completed form. The range of world-class skills available locally made the yard a world-beater able to rise to every technical challenge.

Alas, the craft expertise for which Clydebank was renowned the world over for a century or more is no longer utilised either for shipbuilding or for offshore oil fabrication work. The defunct yard is now the focus of an ambitious scheme that, over fifteen years, is intended to provide housing and retail business developments. Perhaps along the way space may be allocated for the now obligatory heritage museum. Clydebank's achievements and contribution to Scotland's great industrial past may then be celebrated by nostalgic future generations.

Ronnie McDonald

Above The UIE yard contained many obvious remnants of the former John Brown Shipyard.

Right
Sketch 1992
conté and pastel

September 1987

I got up early and walked down to Hyndland station for the train to Clydebank. From my carriage window I could see the old Finneston cranes lining the banks of the Clyde where once the shipyards were located. Unlike the young construction yards set in the rural, remote Highlands, the remaining Clyde shipyards are steeped in industrial Scottish history.

It was still early as I walked down the deserted dual carriageway beside John Brown's shipyard, now UIE. I peered through the locked, rusting, high gates of the neighbouring site, an area of scrub wasteland awaiting enterprise zone developments. This flattened ground used to house numerous communities: tenement homes and local pubs, shops for the shipyard workers. It began to pour with rain and I made my way to the UIE main gate where I was directed to the personnel office. I was welcomed by Lesley, secretary to the industrial relations officer, Alistair Macallum. A bubbly plump blond, Lesley had worked in the office for twelve years. She told me of the depression and unemployment in the area. The Singer factory had recently closed down and the future of this yard was bleak. They were running at 20 per cent capacity.

Allan, the security and safety officer, a young, strongly-built Glaswegian, walked in with a hard hat and boots for me to wear during our walkabout. On site there were five docking berths and seven shops remaining. We walked to the east yard fabrication shops where there were still the old existing buildings from the shipbuilding era, the old time clock hanging on the outside of one of the working sheds and the berth where QE2 was built.

Good News at Clydebank 1993 colour etching

Inside this shop was huge machinery for working with metal: guillotines, saws, cutters and rollers standing in a dark void. Over at berth number one, a small module was the only order to occupy the dwindling workforce. The men were very lively, shouting and whistling as we passed by. Allan told me that the company would have to turn to a care and maintenance stance if no new orders were won. In 1986, 1,600 men plus subcontractors were on the payroll; by 1987 there were only 86 plus subcontractors.

Marathon's jack-up rig, Mr Mac, which had been launched by the Queen in August 1986, still stood on the Clyde, unsold. Two weeks after the royal events many men had been issued with redundancy payments. It was not hard to imagine the yard's working activity during its height in the past, thousands of men in their flat caps and their steel-capped boots. There had been strong resistance to the introduction of hard hats when they were introduced but these had soon taken on their own identities, each trade having a different-coloured hat.

We walked to the empty west fabrications shops; at the far end two men, Frank Fleming and Douglas Adam, were sweeping the clean concrete floor. It seemed emblematic: two men who had spent all their lives working in the yard here now brushing dust. We waited for a car to pick us up in one of the tea huts where pin-up girls shared wall space with the Queen and Duke of Edinburgh calendar. All told me that the artist Stephen Conroy's father worked in the yard. Stephen is one of the 'Glasgow Boys' whose work became famous in the 1980s. His father was very good at drawing cartoons and his work could be seen in many of the portacabins on site.

Clydebank welders wearing their distinctive kromer hats.

Back in the office Lesley called two of the workers up to speak to me, Dunkie Dimick, a welder now laid off, and Robert Dickie, second in charge of stores. Tears of laughter and sadness welled in their eyes as they went over the characters and
stories from the yard. Welders, platers, cokers, burners, shipwrights and carpenters, generations of families who had worked in the yard: Big Wick, 6'2" tall with white thick white hair; Baldy the Toff who was very polite and always joked, 'What have you got that I have not' and then took off his hat; Goose, always goosing; Weather Cock who was constantly on the move and changing his position; Dancer who had a more colourful love life than anyone else; and Squeak who was the playboy. They also talked of segregation between the Catholic and Protestant workers. I had noticed the segregated primary and secondary schools in the area.

Allan drove me back to Queen's Street station. He told me that I had brightened up their day and I promised I would go back soon when they won a big order and see all the men working in every shop.

Kromer Hat Clydebank District Council Residency 1991/3

Sue Jane Taylor returned to UIE yard at Clydebank and set up a makeshift studio in a portacabin. There were many kent faces, and her time there as a lone woman in such a gutsy man's world has been the spice of banter, which has always enlivened her goodhearted rapport with the construction workers. Many men sat for her sketches. Working through the day with charcoal and graphite, acrylic and pastels, she waited until the men had gone home for the night then scoured the yard for dust rust and slivers of steel fine enough to blend into her drawings as part of the texture of their working life.

Finally she chose the welder, Roy Callaghan, to be the model for her portrait bust of 'The Man of the Clyde'. Likeness there may be, but he is meant to be a symbolic figure, much larger than life, dignified by a foursquare heroic simplicity. At the same time she has avoided that Stalinist brutality which diminishes so much of Eastern Europe's portrayal of honest toil. This is a human being, like Josef Herman's coal miners or the industrial peasants sketched by Van Gogh in the Borinage. And even nearer home, the Port Glasgow shipyard workers chronicled so vividly by Stanley Spencer in his wartime paintings.

Look at the man's collar. Its feminine triangular form softens the severe masculine image, but it could be the bows of a ship cleaving the waves. Then the curious motif at his breast – a badge or brooch or a clasp – the artist's own abstracted decoration, which could be the conjunction of a spiraling waveform, a slick of oil and the H-section of a steel girder.

Untitled 1993 acrylic on paper

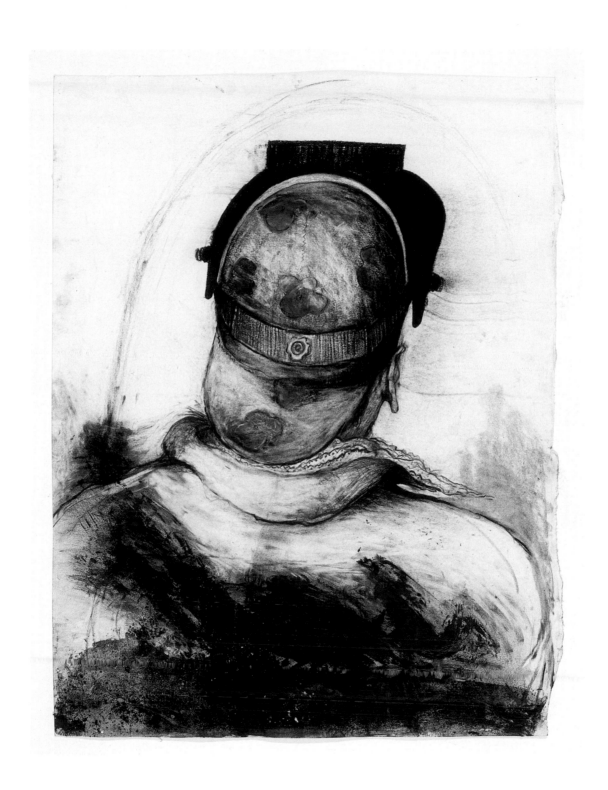

Kromer Hat 1993 charcoal and conté with found objects from workshop floor

Welder 1993 charcoal and conté

An essential part of Sue Jane Taylor's symbolism is the welder's hat, successor to the ubiquitous Clydeside bunnet. It is called a 'kromer' hat and comes by devious routes from Milwaukee. It is fireproof, its peak can be swiveled round to protect the worker's neck from sparks, and it cushions the head against the hard plastic straps of the welding visor. That's the plain technical specification. Macho Clydebank, home of the legendary hard men, has gone gallus with the kromer. The decorated hats have become each man's badge and testament of his individuality. The murmur of one man's discreet Paisley pattern is challenged by the outrageous psychedelic shriek of his mate's. Colour moved through muted pastel to raucous fluorescent. Beneath their rainbows of sparks the helmeted welders are caparisoned like medieval knights. And bandanas worn at the neck flutter like favours tied to jousting lances.

The sculpture has been built up in plaster on a steel armature then carved and rubbed down to the finished form. It has been cast in bronze and patinated to look like rusting steel. The decoration on this Clydebank kromer has no swagger about it, nothing brash or noisy. Delicately it suggests the four petals of a rose, the poet Hugh MacDiarmid's 'little white rose of Scotland that smells sharp and sweet –- and breaks the heart'.

W. Gordon Smith,
Scotland on Sunday Arts Review 1994, and Kromer Hat, Clydebank
Libraries and Museums Department publication.

The artist's residency at UIE Clydebank was supported by the STUC, Dunbartonshire Enterprise and John Brown Engineering UIE (Scotland) Ltd.

Artist working in her makeshift studio in the welding shop in 1992.
ARTIST PORTRAIT: MURDO MACLEOD

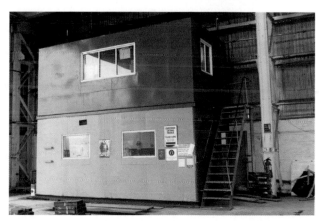

As each ship was completed at John Brown's shipyard every department traditionally had a group photo taken. At the end of her residency at UIE, the artist (centre) celebrated this tradition with the welders of MB5. PHOTO: BILL RUSSELL

Kromer Hat 1993 cast bronze and riveted iron plinth

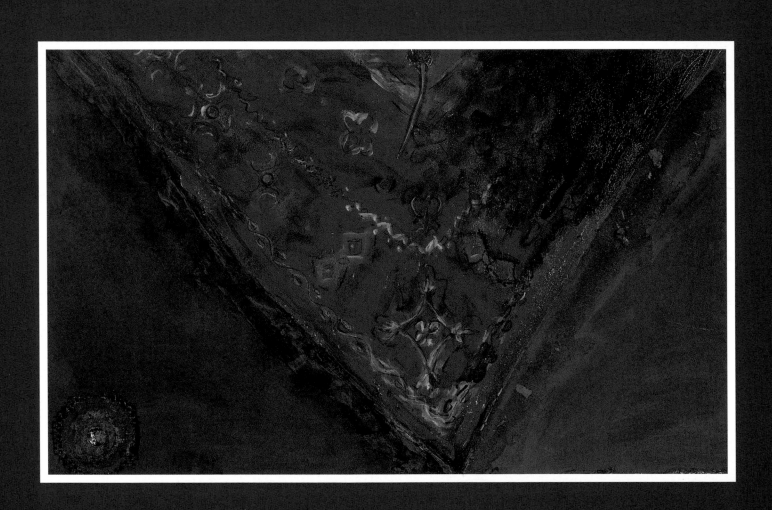

Ray's Bandana 1993 mixed media and found objects from the work shop

ON REVISITING A SCOTTISH RIVER

And call they this Improvement? – to have changed,
my native Clyde, thy once romantic shore,
where Nature's face is banish'd and estranged,
and heaven reflected in thy wave no more;
whose banks, that sweeten'd May-day's breath before,
lie sere and leafless now in summer's beam,
with sooty exhalations cover'd o'er;
and for the daisied green-sward, down thy stream
unsightly brick-lanes smoke, and clanking engines gleam.

Thomas Campbell, 1827

From GLASGOW SONNETS

The North Sea oil-strike tilts Scotland up,
and the great sick Clyde shivers in its bed.
But elegists can't hang themselves on fled -
from trees or poison a recycled cup –
If only a less faint, shaky sunup
glimmered through the skeletal shop and shed
and men washed round the piers like gold and spread
golder in soul than Mitsubishi or Krupp –
The images are ageless but the thing
is now. Without my images the men
ration their cigarettes, their children cling
to broken toys, their women wonder when
the doors will bang on laughter and a wing
over the firth be simply joy again.

Edwin Morgan, 1972

Stirling Shipping was set up by the Harrison family of Glasgow in 1974 to specialise in offshore oil supply ships. At that time Britain's deep-sea merchant fleet was in decline, squeezed both by changing trends in world trade and by competition from flags-of-convenience operators. Harrisons, one of Scotland's older shipping dynasties, nevertheless saw opportunities for a new design of specialised cargo ship to serve the emerging offshore oil and gas industry.

The offshore supply ship is configured differently from other cargo ships because of the way it trades. An 'ordinary' cargo ship is designed to load cargo in port, transport it to another port, and there discharge it whilst berthed alongside. The offshore supply ship, on the other hand, must be capable of loading and offloading out on the high seas alongside oil and gas production platforms and drilling rigs – even in the most inclement weather conditions. The flat-topped box-like design of these ships belies their excellent sea worthiness and station-keeping qualities. Ample power, conveyed through twin screws and bow thrusters, enables position to be maintained precisely under the rig cranes throughout cargo transfer operations.

Cargoes carried on deck include everything required to keep an oilfield functioning from drill pipes to provisions for the rig crews. Bulk tanks below deck carry fuel oil, fresh water and barite for making mud. Drilling mud is critical for the safety of the oil well as it prevents a blow-out of high-pressure gas. Extreme pressures in the oil and gas reservoirs deep below the seabed are equalised by the weight of the column of mud within the well bore. Constant replenishment of this mud from the onboard storage tanks of supply ships like *Stirling Albion* is essential for the safe production of oil and gas from offshore oilfields.

Secor, the American shipping conglomerate, purchased Stirling Shipping's 12-ship fleet in 2002.

Ronnie McDonald

Crude oil from Nigg
terminal, on glass.
PHOTO: FIN MACRAE

Above
Stirling Albion moored at Pocra
Quay, Aberdeen.
Middle
Sketch, York Place 1988 graphite
Below
Dave's Stove 1988 conté and pastel

August/September 1988

Isa Gorst, a journalist for the Petroleum Economist, and I went
aboard at Pocra Quay where the Stirling Albion was moored.
It was a wild, dark evening and the harbour spotlights were very
dim. The captain, Angus Murray, a dark-haired, slightly built Lewis
man, helped us onboard showing us to our cabin next to the galley.
The ship was deserted and silent, as all the men were enjoying
themselves onshore. Only a young Glaswegian sailor, Peter, was
onboard, on night-watch duty. Angus showed us around the vessel;
the sleeping and living quarters were all contained and condensed
at the front of the ship. These vessels were not designed for the
comfort of the crew, cargo is king: three quarters of the ship's area
was taken up by cargo, with huge storage tanks positioned below
the deck. The ship was larger than the *Stirling Teal*, which I had
sailed on in 1984 on my first offshore trip, and Angus warned me
that in rough waters it was not as sympathetic to its passengers
as the *Teal*.

I set up my tripod and camera and began to take some shots of
the ship and neighbouring moored ships in the quay: no one was
around, just the wind whistling its way into the harbour.

I woke to the smell of breakfast cooking next door. Dave the cook, a
quiet, dark Glaswegian, was busy at work. Memories of my *Teal* trip
flooded back: when, on the rough seas, I had sat and watched
Jimmy the cook preparing three-course meals whilst the vessel
was listing from side to side, up and down, rolling; the pots and
pans were hooked onto the sides of the cooker for security.

After breakfast I climbed up to the bridge where I met more of the
crew: Colin, the second mate from Fleetwood, and Bald Eagle, third
mate. Whilst Bald Eagle was writing up the log, I drew him. He told
me we were not sailing until the next day because an oil company
had requested another item of cargo.

I got up early and stepped out onto the deck where the dockers were loading. I found a safe spot and started to draw the scene in front of me, the crane lifting the huge cargo containers. At 2.50 pm we set sail. As we passed the harbour walls and sailed out into the open sea, the boat started to rock and roll with the big swell of sea. This was hard to adjust to, just as it had been on the *Stirling Teal* journey before.

I decided to rest, rocked to sleep, until we reached our first destination at 3 am, the semi-submersible oilrig, DF19 Dixie Field. I struggled up to the captain's bridge where Angus was operating the ship's controls whilst the crane of the rig was unloading its allotted cargo off the ship. Bald Eagle was also on watch. Looking down onto the deck the two sailors were hooking on the cargo load for lifting and directing the returned cargo from the rig. These operations were extremely dangerous as they tried to avoid the swirl of the sea as it swept along the deck. Isa came up for a short while but soon retired.

After breakfast I took some photos. It was now daylight and the swell of the sea against the ship and rig was spectacular. On deck Angus was trying to persuade the rig that it would be too difficult to load cement into tanks at the front of the ship, as this would mean laying the hose across the ship's deck whilst loading and the ship was not built for this job. Finally the rig gave in. Angus told me that dangerous requests from platforms and rigs were not unusual.

The supply vessels were expected to be at their beck and call and to operate in the stormiest of weathers. Angus said he was going to take early retirement. He had worked on the sea all his life, firstly in the merchant navy and then in the oil industry. He was tired of the long arduous hours and 'summers seem more often like winters in the North Sea' according to him. I retired to my bunk and slept until Dave woke me for supper. Looking out of the mess porthole it was, in Angus's words, 'moderate to rough'. I could not see any moderation.

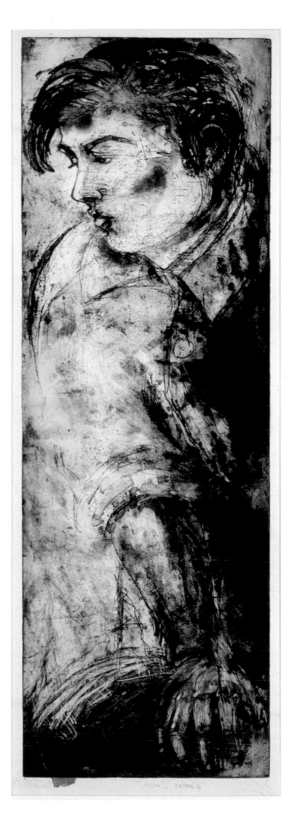

Laurie's Catch 1989 colour etching with chine collé

Angus 1989 colour etching with chine collé

We arrived at Montrose Alpha and I sat up on the bridge and looked out at the bright orange platform standing out against the beautiful evening sky. Colin accompanied me down on to the deck where I could sketch and take shots of the sailors working close at hand.

Being close to the water was exhilarating, looking down into its dark unfriendly depths with the salt water hitting me as it splashed the sides of the ship. The cargo was unloaded and we sailed off to Rowan Gorilla II, a jack-up rig, half an hour's sailing time away. I took black and white infrared shots of the sailors helping to load equipment weighing eight tons each onto the ship's deck in stormy seas. Operations were complete by midnight.

I watched a Bruce Lee film with Davy before going to bed. In my bunk I could feel the ship dodging up and down all night, its waves smacking and bashing against its stern: the noise of the engines was constant and the smell of the chemicals from the tanks wafted around the galley and our cabin.

In the morning we returned to Montrose field to pick up cargo and I spent some time on deck again. On our return journey I felt unwell, mainly due to tiredness, and had to lie down in my bunk. Isa felt better; she had found her sea legs. At 10.30 pm we docked at Aberdeen and all the men rushed off to the pub. Angus had gone to bed and Billy was on night watch; he teased me for having to lie down on the return journey.

On the last morning we all had breakfast together. It was a beautiful morning so I lined the crew up on the quay alongside their ship for a group photo - every one of them characters, strong men enduring their extreme work and lifestyle.

Above
Gadus morhua (cod) 1989 pastel and watercolour

Middle Offshore night loading on deck infrared

Below (left to right) Stirling Albion crew, lorry drivers and Miller Platform.

Approaching the Rig 1985 colour etching

Rough Seas II 1985 colour etching

Untitled 1989 mixed media with gold pigment

OVERDUE

O ragin' wind
An' cruel sea,
Ye put the fear
O' daith on me.
I canna sleep,
I canna pray,
But prowl aboot
The docks a' day,
An' pu' my plaid
Aboot me ticht.
'Nae news yet, mistress!'
Ae mair night!

Helen B. Cruickshank,
1934

From BIRLINN CHLANN RAGHNAILL

'N uiar thuiteamaid fo bharr

Nan ardthonn giobach,
Cur beag nach dochainneadh a sail,
An t-aigeal sligneach.

An fhairge 'g a maistreadh 's 'g a sluistreadh
Troimh a cheile,
Gu'n robh roin is mialan mora
Am barrachd eiginn'.

Alasdair Mac Mhaighstir Alasdair c. 1760

When she would plunge from towering summits
     down pell-mell
almost the ship's heel would be bruised
     by the sea-floor's shells,

the ocean churning, mixing, stirring
     its abyss,
seals and huge sea creatures howling
     in distress.

Alexander MacDonald

10. SULLOM VOE OIL TERMINAL Shetland Isles 1989

Its name, Sullom Voe (Old Norse for *Bay of the Gannet*), attests as much to the richness of the natural environment as it does to the Viking heritage of the Shetlanders. For millennia before the arrival of Norwegian farmers ancient Pictish peoples prospered, sustained by the sea's abundance.

In 1448 Shetland was pledged to Scotland in part-payment of a dowry on the marriage of Margaret of Denmark to Scotland's James III. On the ascension of James VI to the English throne in 1603, Shetland became part of the United Kingdom. And so it came about that the vast oil wealth under the North Sea, discovered in 1970, fell to a relieved British nation to exploit.

Sullom Voe was chosen as the site of the main oil terminal to gather the oil coming ashore from fifteen oilfields in the East Shetland Basin, mid-way between Shetland and Norway. The oil is pumped ashore through a grid of pipelines laid on the sea floor. A natural harbour, the Voe is ideal for loading ocean-going super tankers. Construction of the terminal, complete with four loading jetties, storage tanks, pumping stations and separators for extracting the gas from the oil took seven years to complete. Sullom Voe was the biggest construction project in Europe employing at its peak some 7,000 men and women. By 1981 the terminal was handling 75 per cent of UK oil exports.

Uniquely, the people of Shetland are set to continue to benefit from oil long after the wells offshore have dried up. A local tax is exacted on every ton of oil shipped out of the Voe by virtue of a special Act of Parliament passed in 1974 giving this power to the local authority. Tens of millions of pounds have been accumulated by the fund for the benefit of the Islanders. As a consequence, sports facilities, social amenities, and provision of care for the elderly are among the very best in Europe.

The terminal at Sullom Voe continues to tranship oil to world markets and oil from new oilfields in the western approaches of the Atlantic will also make landfall at Sullom Voe.

Ronnie McDonald

Opposite
Crude oil from
Nigg terminal,
on copper plate.
PHOTO: FIN MACRAE

November 1989

My first glimpse of the Shetland Isles came with
our flight's descent towards Scatsa. Beneath me was
a rugged, craggy landscape covered with heather
interspersed with green croft land. To the right the
Sullom Voe terminal sat as a firm fixture on the
landscape; it seemed vast compared to Flotta.
Two tankers were docked at its jetty while giant gas
flares burned in the background. As I surveyed the
sheer vastness of Sullom Voe I caught a snippet of an
oilman's conversation. Talking to his mate he said of
Shetland: 'This has got to be the coldest place on earth.'

At the small airport terminal I phoned for a taxi to drive
me to Lerwick to pick up my hired car. The twenty-six-
mile drive past lots of lochs with small circular fish
cages for trout and salmon farming was on very good
two-way roads with hardly any single track to be seen.
The harbour was very busy with BP and Shell industrial
sites, supply vessels, stacks and rows of drilling rods
and klondikers in for repair. The centre of town was
similar to Stromness, with narrow, winding, flagstone
streets. One could smell the peat-burning fires and fish
landed at the port.

Above *Bonny* 1989 graphite
Right *Sketch* 1989 pastel and pen

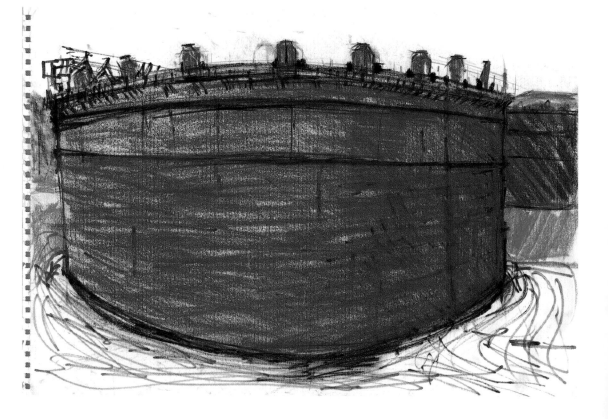

The aftermath of Shetland's 'Gold Rush'.

I drove past the busy Sumburgh airport and heliport up to Sumburgh Head lighthouse and looked over the cliffs. Lots of guillemots were flying, gliding and swooping below. I could see a girl on a horse galloping along the white/grey sandy beach in the distance. It was dark as I drove to Mossbank where Mrs Griffith runs the B&B. I passed Sullom Voe on the way, its huge torches, gas flares, burnt against the dark sky. Mrs Griffith had come to Shetland in 1977 with her husband who worked on the construction of the terminal. For a time they had lived on a barge. The islands had been ill-prepared for the huge influx of construction workers. Many workers had been reduced to sleeping in the back seats of their cars. For many months a throng of tightly-packed caravans had dotted the landscape.

In the morning I made my way to Fraser Peterson Centre, what was left of the construction village. It was the first in Shetland to be built for the workers at the terminal. It had an almost ghostly presence with no evidence of the village remaining, only water tanks and drainage systems. Looking over at the other village site, Firth Construction village, there seemed to be more buildings still standing, and a green patch of land where sheep now grazed against the peat land.

Inside the derelict buildings were strewn beds and mattresses, dead sheep and old television sets. In what was once a bar, the floor was filling up with sheep wool and droppings; torn images of country and western stars and pin-ups lay mouldering on the dirt-caked floor. Men had bought beer here, at this bar as long as a bus, for as little as ten pence a pint.

Accommodation cabin doors swung wildly in the wind and the tattered, torn curtains clung on at the windows. The games hall used by the workers is now a community centre. When the camps closed down the locals were free to take what they wanted: furniture, fittings, wood, shower units, radiators, etc. Tractors and trailers from all over the island rolled up.

Six thousand construction workers lived in these two camps with their facilities. Big bands and entertainers were frequent visitors. I remember as a teenager wanting to go and work as a cleaner in these camps, for the money offered was incredible by normal standards, but my mother thought it too risky. The caravan site at Hillswick gained special notoriety for the rough lifestyle of its inhabitants.

Annie Scott, now head teacher of a north coast primary school in Sutherland, worked as a chambermaid at Firth Camp back in 1975. As she told me, in the Firth Camp the chambermaids made up a 'Guide to Survival' in order to avoid being knocked out by fumes when cleaning the men's sleeping quarters:

Step 1: Open both emergency exits. Let the wind sweep through the block.

Step 2: Unlock each room, holding nose. Dash across the room to the window, fling it open and retreat quickly.

Step 3: Do not be distracted by lewd literature strewn around, or by messages written in shaving cream on the mirror.

Step 4: When the hurricane force of the Shetland wind has done its job, it is safe to finish off the rooms.

Warning: Retreat quickly to the next block if a raging bull, who might have just been sacked and told to collect his belongings, enters the block.

Sea of Gold 1989 mixed media with gold pigment

I drove to the terminal to meet Pearl MacGrath, BP's external affairs assistant. Pearl was born and bred in Yell. She gave me a guided tour of the thousand-acre site in the company's Range Rover. We drove past the storage tanks for crude oil from the Brent and Ninian fields, known as the tank farm.

We later watched a tanker dock at the jetty, flanked by an escort of two pilot tugs. We went to look at the tanker, *Bonny*, a vessel of monstrous proportions. The ship's deck extended further than two football pitches combined. The Finnish crew featured some real characters, not least the captain himself who invited us on board. A handsome, formidably built man, he ushered Pearl and me into his cabin for a nip of Arctic Berry, a Finnish liqueur. Later, he showed us around his immaculate vessel.

After we returned to base we saw a pair of ravens hovering near the booms for the flares up on the moors. The raven is but one of an estimated 145 species of birds which, along with the ever-playful otters, have managed to survive and thrive despite the intrusion of this massive industrial site.

Reflecting on the images of the giant tankers docking and departing from the jetty I could almost believe that only two of these tankers, fully loaded with crude, carry the equivalent of Britain's daily petroleum demand. It seemed a cruelly unfair irony that Shetland motorists pay the highest petrol prices in Britain.

Thousands of transient workers came and left in a rush.

Tank Farm Sullom Voe 1989 pen and ink wash with pastel

Fish 1989
watercolour and pastel

Pearl and her husband Ian picked me up in the evening and drove me to two pubs, Hillswick and Booth. At Booth we sat and chatted over a whisky, warming ourselves by the fire. Jan, the proprietor, had a seal rescue centre at the back of the pub and we fed the rescued and injured seals with some fish heads; she also had an injured otter.

Next day I walked around the terminal site drawing details of the vast industrial landscape. Shetland seems to have really benefited from the oil. There are numerous facilities in each village and there is still a strong sense of community, because the people still own the land the oil terminal was built on.

'Stormy Seas II'

A/P   Sae Tan FH '15.

Rough Seas III 1985 etching

She's a solan, she's a tramper, she's a sea-shaker,
she's a hawk, she's a hammer, she's a big-sea-breaker,
she's a falcon, she's a kestrel, she's a wide-night-seeker,
she's a river, she's a render, she's a foam-spray-waker.
She's a stieve sea-strider, she's a storm-course-keeper,
she's a tide-scour-bucker, she's a quick-light-leaper,
she's a stem-tearer, keel-tearer, seeker, finder, reaper.
She's Cast off! Anchor up! Deid anchor-weary,
she's a chain-snubber, moorin'-strainer, restless herbour peerie.
She's a skyline-raiser, skyline-sinker, hulldown horizon-crosser,
She's foreland foreland, on and on, a high-heid-tosser.
She's a glint, she's a glimmer, she's a glimpse, she's a fleeter,
she's an overhauler, leave-astern, a hale-fleet-beater;
she's a kyle-coulter, knot-reeler, thrang-speed-spinner,
her mood is moulded on her and the mind that made her's in her.
She's a wake-plough, foam-plough, spray hammer, roarer,
she's a wind-anvil, crest-batterer, deep-trough-soarer,
she's a dance-step-turner, she's a broad-wake-scorer,
She's a sound-threider, bight-stringer, her hert runs oot afore her.
When the big long seas come on lik walls, cold-white-heided,
she doesna flinch a point for them. Straight her wake is threaded.

George Campbell Hay, 1948

11. PIPER ALPHA DISASTER 1988–91

I was living in London when I heard the terrible news on the radio about the Piper Alpha explosion. I could not believe it. Over a year ago I had been on that platform. My first thoughts were for the men I had got to know on my trip offshore; had they survived the explosive fire? It was hard to conceive how anybody could have escaped alive from such a burning inferno as that which I saw on the television pictures.

In the weeks following the disaster I was invited to the headquarters of Occidental, the owners of the platform. They had heard that I was about to have an exhibition with some works from my Piper Alpha visit. The Public Relations manager ushered me into his office. This was a man whom I had met on several previous occasions, but from the look on his face and by his body language I could see that he was now under a great deal of pressure and strain. His job seemed to be to try to suppress any publicity concerning Piper Alpha from recent visitors to the platform.

He proposed that instead of going ahead with my touring exhibition, 'Oil Worker Scotland', which was about to open in the autumn at the City Art Centre in Edinburgh, the company should buy all of my work. I could name my price. I was to wrap them all up and bring them to head office. He also wanted to scrutinise all the images which I had photographed, drawn or recorded on the platform. I did not know it at the time but they were looking for evidence of any kind which might be held against the company and make them liable in a future inquiry. I could only answer that I needed time to think. The company had never before shown the slightest interest in my work, but I had now become a very minor potential threat in that I might keep the name of Piper alive in the public eye.

I learnt that some of the dead were men I had met and drawn on my visit to Piper. I needed desperately to speak to someone close to the disaster but on the other side of the fence for advice. I also felt I needed some legal advice should the company start applying pressure. Aberdeen City Council had appointed a group of social workers, the Piper Alpha Outreach Team, to assist with counselling the bereaved families and survivors and anyone affected by the disaster. Whilst I was in Aberdeen working on the final series of the prints for 'Oil Worker Scotland' at Peacock Printmakers, I contacted the Outreach Team's office and did receive some counselling from them. On a visit to their office I met one of the survivors, Bob Ballantayne, who remembered seeing me on the platform during my visit but had not liked to speak to me as he'd thought I was one of 'Oxy's people'.

Opposite
Artist's luggage tag
in 1988.

Bob was going through incredible mood swings such as only a survivor of the disaster could feel and describe. He showed me his paintings which he was holding in his hand at the time: intense burning fires, spreading right out to every corner and edge of the paper, his living nightmare of being a survivor. These paintings were part of his healing process, facing his nightmares.

It was arranged that I should meet some of the relatives and survivors to ask their opinion about my work. It became clear that there was a very positive consensus in showing the works: they regarded these works as part of a visual memorial to the men who perished that night. In my reply to Occidental I therefore stated my intention to go ahead and show my work, a letter which I took legal advice in writing. I was very nervous as I knew what corporate oil giants could get up to if they did not get their own way and I was still stunned by their attitude to me.

Many of the bereaved families and survivors attended the opening night of the exhibition in Edinburgh, giving their support to my show. The show went on tour in twelve venues throughout the country, and to my surprise generated considerable media interest, something I would have to get used to whilst working on the Memorial.

Sketch for Memorial 1990 acrylic and pastel

An Crann Dubh (The Black Tree) 1989 colour etching

Piper Alpha Memorial

The bereaved families set up a memorial committee to organise a fundraising appeal for the total cost of a memorial to the dead men. They also started looking for a suitable artist to liaise with and create the artwork: a lasting visual memorial, a focus and homage for those families whose loved ones' bodies were never found. Along with a number of other artists, I was approached by members of the committee to submit ideas. I had never tackled anything on this scale before or of such public high profile. Several factors were in my favour, however, notably that for the past five years my work had been involved with the North Sea industry and the fact that a year before the Piper Alpha disaster I had met and drawn some of the men who had died. I dearly wanted the commission. I felt very personally involved; it was as if all my visual work and experience in visiting these oil-related sites was in preparation for this work

Once the committee had chosen me to carry out the work, the first step was to create a maquette model of the memorial to be approved by the arts and recreation committee of Aberdeen City Council. The memorial committee had a set brief: three figures symbolizing the platform's workforce offshore. Importantly for the families, the plinth, on which the figures would stand, would prominently profile all the names of the men who perished that night. (The material for the plinth, Pink Corrennie locally quarried at Tillyfourie, Aberdeenshire, was donated by John Fyfe Granite Works, Aberdeen).

Above *Untitled* 1988   charcoal and conté

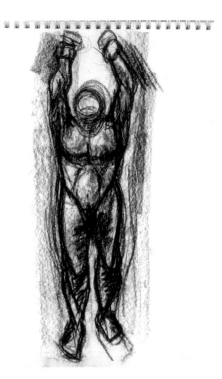
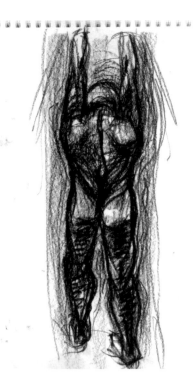

Below left and above *Preparatory drawings for Piper Alpha Memorial* 1990.

Meanwhile, in the background, the politics were getting nasty. Occidental was stating that it was very much against a memorial and that the book of remembrance placed in the Aberdeen City Art Gallery, which was their own contribution, should be the lasting memory for the men. Their attitude generated disbelief in the bereaved families. Many requests were made to the company, including one from Bob Ballantayne, who asked Occidental to donate the scrap value of the recovered accommodation module in which many deceased men had been found. Occidental refused. It was also placing pressure behind the scenes on its fellow oil companies in the North Sea not to contribute to the fund appeal. This became apparent when only £14,000 was donated from all the oil companies

operating in the North Sea: seven did not reply to the memorial committee and the remainder donated sums ranging from a maximum of £2,000 down to £150. Many individuals donated funds but £100,000 was the target. To save embarrassment the Conservative Government had to step in with help of public money in the name of the Scottish Office in the region of £40,000.

I moved to the Scottish Sculpture Workshop in the village of Lumsden, Aberdeenshire which has facilities to carry out large-scale works and technical back-up for commissions such as these. The workshop is an open facility founded by sculptor Fred Bush for visiting artists and is mostly used by people from overseas.

Above, below and opposite
Preparatory drawings for Piper Alpha Memorial 1990.

First, I created a series of large working drawings, in conté and charcoal, investigating the pose for each of the three figures. These were drawn from life models, each chosen for his age and features: one was an Aberdeen University arts graduate, the son of the workshop's secretary; one was a visiting sculptor at the workshop; and the third was a survivor, Bill Barron.

I was very conscious of the figures' movement and form but also very aware of 'drapes': the offshore uniforms worn by the men. Bill Barron was a great help in knowing what the men usually wore in their work offshore and we visited various oil companies whose work-clothing we borrowed, such as a survival suit, hat, boots and boiler suits.

It was tough working out at rural Lumsden with its basic living conditions, no real comforts and distractions, just keeping one's mind focused on the job. I also sensed that certain circles of the Scottish art establishment were very sceptical about my abilities to do the job, primarily because I was not in a traditional sense of the word a 'sculptor'. This spurred me on. It was also stimulating to work in such a cosmopolitan atmosphere with artists from all over the world staying periodically. I remember that for all the resident artists one highlight of the week in the winter was the television serialisation of David Lynch's *Twin Peaks*.

In the early stages there was no guarantee that the funds for the memorial would be found. I attended regular meetings with the families' committee. These were at times emotionally charged and stressful. I tried as much as I could to keep my distance from anything other than working on the memorial because I knew that there were pressures on the committee from all sides and I had to focus. These were hurt, grieving people.

Once I had a firm idea of how the figures' stance and positioning would be I created a three-dimensional maquette. The council officially approved the model and the families were offered two locations for the memorial: Rubislaw Gardens in the centre of Aberdeen or a site in Hazelhead Park on the outskirts of the city. The families opted for the quieter and more reflective site in Hazelhead Park where a rose garden surrounding the sculpture would be especially landscaped.

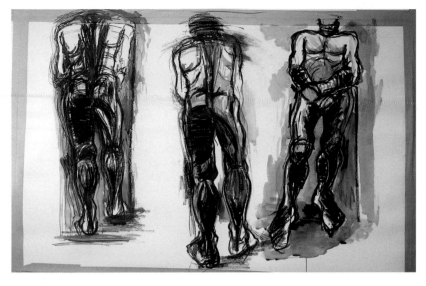

Above *Maquette (scaled model) for Piper Alpha Memorial* 1990.
Below *Plaster study for central figure.*

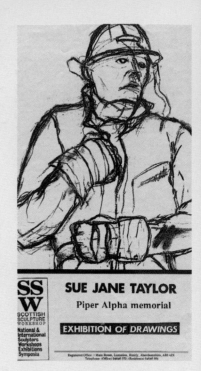

SUE JANE TAYLOR

Piper Alpha memorial

EXHIBITION OF DRAWINGS

I got the go-ahead to work on the final figures but time was running out, with only nine months to complete the whole project, including a three-month period of bronze casting. The unveiling date was 6 July, the anniversary of the disaster. I began to live and breathe the commission.

I increased my working scale for the figures as a test piece with steel armatures, working in clay, but I was still not convinced that this was the most appropriate medium to work with. It was insufficiently flexible and had to be kept moist. After discussion with other artists staying at the time, the most suitable and versatile material seemed to be plaster.

I created my own personal working environment in one of the big outside sheds. It was single wall, unrendered breeze-block with the water dripping through the walls when it rained or snowed. I tried to create a protective cocoon by stapling bubble wrap over the draughty, large, creaking wooden doors. The technicians, who were sculptors themselves, assisted me with the steel armature to the correct one and a half times larger than life size and I started working on the first and central figure.

Bill Barron drove out every day from Aberdeen and posed for me with his spaniel sitting by his side. Whilst I worked on the piece Bill would tell me stories from his days in the army or during his time working in England, cleaning and painting the colossal cooling towers of power stations. He also spoke of his escape from the burning platform. The official safety procedures in an emergency were to assemble and wait for a helicopter to rescue the men. But like other survivors Bill knew that no helicopter would land on the burning installation. He climbed down a rope and hung on until he could see a rescue vessel and jumped into the sea.

Above Gary, Bill and the artist at work in the studio.
Below By tea-break, Jim was frequently exhausted by the heat.

He could not swim but had a lifejacket on to keep him afloat until he was picked up. Feelings of guilt ran very deep within him and it was difficult for him to talk much about it. But we had also some great laughs and he remembered me visiting the platform, wondering 'what the hell' a young woman was doing drawing on the platform.

For the roustabout figure my model, Gary, who was waiting to get into the Royal College of Art in London to study post-graduate sculpture, built a pulley system hanging from the rafters for resting his arms on: it was impossible for him to hold the pose without this support. He looked like a puppet on a string.

Jim, the young arts graduate, also brought his little dog along with him. Jim suffered in the heat of the summer, wearing his sweaty survival suit all day during modelling. He used to love telling me about the books he was reading; *Ulysses* by Joyce was his hot favourite.

The winter months, with dark days and very cold conditions, was the testing period for me. On one occasion whilst working in my shed on my own in December with two huge gas burners going on either side of me, the temperature inside the shed was minus five degrees. I decided to go to bed to keep warm.

The emotional pressure was at times suffocating with the bereaved families depending on me to create this huge sculpture. During this time I also suffered a tragic family bereavement. I tried to focus on creating a work of art, partly representational in its making, which would be timeless and stand on its own: the rhythms and movements of the figures, their presence, poignancy, symbolism and hope.

Television crews from both Grampian and BBC Scotland would come out at various stages and film the sculpture's progression and nearer the time of unveiling, national television crews would turn up.

Working in the studio (the building on the left) was particularly arduous in winter.

I always had national newspapers on my back interested in taking shots of the sculpture in its working state. Some families and survivors would also visit.

The relief and nervous excitement in witnessing the casting process of the figures at Burleighfield Foundry, High Wycombe over the three-month period was indescribable and even more so seeing the sculpture *in situ* before the official opening. Instead of celebrating the sculpture's completion, however, I was struck down with a bad case of 'flu and was confined to my little room at the workshop in Lumsden. For the first two days I was unable to make my way across the yard to the kitchen and television room. On the third day I heard a knock on the door and it was a visiting Belgian artist carrying a tray of food, manna from Heaven. He told me, in broken English, that this would make me better. It was boiled eggs and salad

displayed like a work of art. That week, during my illness, the phone calls seemed to increase. I would stagger out of bed and stand shivering in the draughty lobby discussing preparations for the Memorial ceremony on the phone. Not my fondest memory of this workshop.

On the warm, calm, sunny day of the unveiling ceremony, twelve buses brought relatives and survivors to Hazelhead Park. Some relatives had flown in from as far afield as Canada and New Zealand. Tight security was in place for the Queen Mother who, in her ninetieth year, unveiled the memorial in front of a thousand invited guests in the newly named North Sea Rose Garden. In the words of Reverend Alan Swinton, chaplain of Aberdeen Royal Infirmary: 'We gather with hurt in our hearts, tears in our eyes and an emptiness inside that time seems hardly to have healed.'

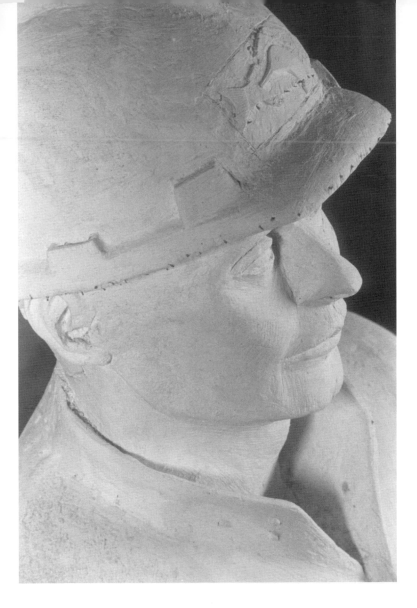

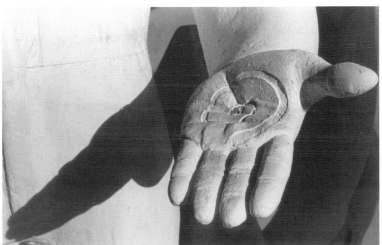

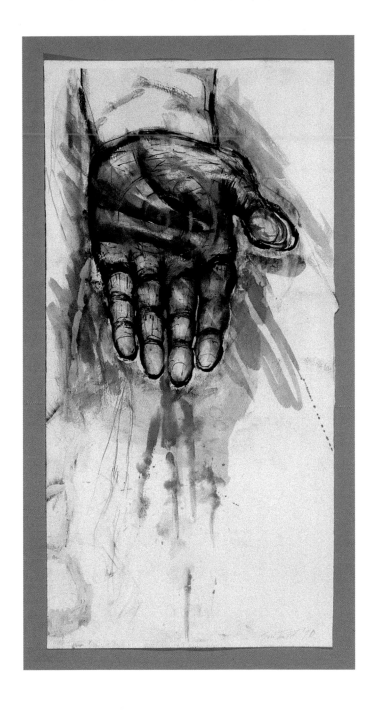

Above *Spiral of Black Gold* 1990 pen and ink wash

Above left *Central figure detail* plaster original
PHOTO: RAY SMITH

Left *Central figure detail of black gold spiral on the left hand*
plaster original PHOTO: RAY SMITH

Above Plaster figures leaving Lumsden.

Below The process of bronze casting at Burleighfield was a complex and intense three-month period.

The Queen Mother in many ways depoliticised the whole evocative occasion. It seemed that she swept away all controversy and her presence meant so much to the families. When she pulled away the drapes covering the figures a quiet gasp could be heard from the gathered congregation. At that point I wanted to melt into the ground, to disappear; the atmosphere was so emotional.

The reception in the park's restaurant after the unveiling, amongst dignitaries, politicians, families and survivors, was a momentous, sad occasion but also a quiet positive step towards the healing process amongst those so closely affected.

The British sector of the North Sea oilfield came to a halt for an hour at noon in respect for those who died and the night-shift paid a similar tribute at 11 pm on the day of the unveiling.

One week after the unveiling Occidental sold all their British interests to Elf, including the Piper field which was renamed Piper Bravo.

Above Burleighfield foundry worker welding on the legs of the bronze survival suit figure.

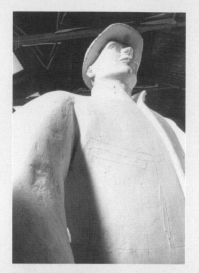

PHOTOS: RAY SMITH

Description of figures

The central bronze figure, which faces north towards the main entrance of the gardens, represents a mature character. In his left hand he holds a pool of oil sculpted in the shape of an unwinding natural spiral form. This black shape in his palm flows into gold leaf. His right hand points down to the ground, indicating the source of the crude oil. The carved motif on his helmet, a fish and seabird design, symbolises the environmental aspects of the oil industry's presence in the North Sea.

The 'roustabout' bronze figure, which faces west, represents the physical nature of many offshore trades. His pose emphasises two opposite 'strain' movements in offshore work: push and pull. On his right sleeve is a 'tree of life' motif, based on the Celtic design. Its leaves are in gold leaf. The design's mythological meanings symbolise the exploration and production of crude oil. For example, its roots deep in the bowels of the earth represent the vast oil wells underneath the sea-bed; the tips of its branches reaching up to the sky, the eternal flame of the flare boom on oil and gas production platforms; the vapour rising into the earth's atmosphere.

The 'survival suit' bronze figure, which faces east, represents youth and eternal movement. On the left sleeve of this figure is a design of a sea eagle's wingspan and its head, gilt in gold leaf. The sea eagle is native to the northern seas, and it is used in place of the North American eagle, the patron of oil.

On the south face of the Memorial plinth, above the Celtic cross, are inscribed the names of the thirty men with no resting place on shore. A casket of unknown ashes is interred behind the cross. On the east face of the plinth are inscribed the names of the two heroic crewmen of the *Sandhaven* rescue vessel.

The gold leaf was applied by Pam Bramley, a visiting Australian artist to the Scottish Sculpture Workshop.

Above left
Survival suit figure detail
bronze
PHOTO: RAY SMITH

Above right
Roustabout figure detail
bronze
PHOTO: RAY SMITH

Right
Roustabout figure detail
bronze with gold leaf
(applied by sculptor Pam Bramley)
PHOTO: RAY SMITH

An Tuireadh Lament, James MacMillan

Molly Pearston from the Piper Alpha Families' Association was very keen to commission a piece of music in memory of the Piper Alpha victims. The body of Molly's son was never found after the disaster. In discussions with Molly, she and I decided to approach a musician/composer to write a piece in memory of the lost men. Having heard on the wireless his awe-inspiring *The Confession of Isobel Gowdie* world premiere at the Proms in London, I suggested that we approach the contemporary Scottish composer, James MacMillan. He agreed to write a tribute for the forthcoming St Magnus Festival in Orkney commissioned by BBC Radio 3 and performed by the Allegri String Quartet in St Magnus Cathedral, Kirkwall. The Piper Alpha Families' Association commissioned a large banner based on my 'survival suit' figure drawing, screen-printed by Peacock Printmakers, Aberdeen, to hang in the cathedral accompanying the piece.

As Macmillan wrote in the Orkney Festival catalogue of June 1991: '*Tuireadh* is Gaelic for a lament (or requiem) for the dead, and the work is dedicated to the victims of the Piper Alpha disaster and their families. It was written as a musical complement to the memorial sculpted by Sue Jane Taylor and placed in Aberdeen. In responding to this I was specifically inspired by a letter sent to me by the mother of one of the dead men, who wrote movingly of her visit to the scene of the memorial service.

This became a rite of passage for those whose loved ones had not been found, and the mother described how a spontaneous keening sound rose gently from the mourners assembled on the boat. The work attempts to capture this outpouring of grief in music and makes allusions to the intervallic and ornamental archetypes of various lament forms from Scottish traditional music.' (The Orkney Festival is part-funded by Occidental.)

Above Banner for *An Tuireadh Lament* in St Magnus Cathedral, Kirkwall
PHOTO: GUNNIE MOBERG

Below *James MacMillan*, Glasgow 1992 conté and pastel

The Queen Mother unveils the Memorial in Hazelhead Park, 6 July 1991. PHOTO: MURDO MACLEOD

"When I go there I kneel down, look up at it from all different angles and levels, stand far back, sit and contemplate. To a survivor and the bereaved it is a terribly potent symbol of that disaster."

Bob Ballantyne (survivor)

The Piper Alpha Memorial, south side. PHOTO: RAY SMITH

BOOM TOON

Ile toon, boom city,
Houston o the North –
sombreros instead o bonnets?
black gowd instead o siller?

Havers! Frae Fittie
tae Rubislaw yer granite
waas'll halt sic an invasion.
The blunt speak o Aiberdonian
doddies winna encompass
yon obligatory drawl.

The smell onywey'll tell
ye. Nae ile – fish!

Ken Morrice, 1979

ABERDEEN

The grey sea turns in its sleep
disturbing seagulls from the green rock.

We watched the long collapse, the black drop
and frothing of the toppled wave; looked out
on the dark that goes to Norway.

We lay all night in an open boat, that rocked
by the harbour wall – listening to the tyres creak
at the stone quay, trying to keep time –
till the night-fishers came in their arc, their lap
of light: the fat slap of waves, the water's
sway, the water mullioned with light.

The sifting rain, italic rain; the smirr
that drifted down for days; the sleet.
Your hair full of hail, as if sewn there.
In the damp sheets we left each other sea-gifts,
watermarks: long lost now in all these years
of the rip-tide's swell and trawl.

All night the feeding storm banked up
the streets and houses. In the morning
the sky was yellow, the frost ringing.

The grey sea turns in its sleep
disturbing seagulls from the green rock.

Robin Robertson, 1997

12. PIPER BRAVO PLATFORM North Sea 2004

While intended to be the safest oil and gas production platform ever built in the UK sector, not everyone welcomed the news in 1989 of Piper Bravo's development. Unresolved anger and grief following the loss of 167 souls on Piper Alpha still distressed the survivors and the grieving families. Those held responsible by the families for the tragedy seemed unable to acknowledge that it had been avoidable; yet, here they were announcing business as usual. It was too much, too soon for many. In the event, the new platform came onstream in 1993 under the control of a new operator, Elf Enterprise, within the framework of new safety regulations born of the Cullen Inquiry into the causes of the Piper Alpha disaster. A new platform; a new beginning.

The Piper Bravo platform sits within sight of the buoy that marks the wreck of Piper Alpha and is everything its predecessor was not. It incorporates every conceivable safety enhancement including free-fall lifeboats able to be launched in a fraction of the time taken to load and lower conventional lifeboats. Process control systems are state of the art and are designed to prevent even the smallest incident escalating into a major event.

Prevention and control are the primary objectives but integral to the platform's design are other defences such as water deluge systems and blast walls able to lessen the consequences of a major fire or explosion should it occur. Comparisons with Piper Alpha are unavoidable and whereas Alpha produced on a daily basis 40 per cent more oil and gas than it had originally been designed for, Bravo, from day one, has been amply engineered to accommodate 24 wells and to handle up to 140,000 barrels per day of oil production.

The eight-legged 51,330 tonnes platform is linked to the seabed pipeline system taking oil and natural gas liquids to the Flotta terminal in Orkney. Gas is transported to St Fergus on the Scottish mainland via another pipeline. In one key respect Piper Bravo represents not just a new generation of offshore production platform, but a new approach to how the remaining oil and gas reserves of the North Sea must be exploited. With half of all oil extracted, and the remaining reserves mostly situated in smaller reservoirs scattered across the continental shelf, Piper Bravo will increasingly function as a hub, gathering hydrocarbons from outlying smaller accumulations, processing them and pumping them to shore.

On 1 May 2000 Talisman Energy took over operating Piper Bravo.

Ronnie McDonald

Piper Bravo
Helideck 2004
infrared

Piper revisited fifteen years later

In 2004 I was invited by Talisman Energy (UK) Ltd, the present owners of the Piper field, to spend five days offshore on Piper Bravo platform, as part of their sponsorship for this book. I had never imagined that I would revisit the field or stay on the new Piper Bravo platform. Would I find it unsettling, disturbing? Would everything have changed dramatically? It was with some trepidation that I accepted the offer.

Extracts from the artist's diary:

Thursday, 30 September

At Scotia heliport I struggled into the large open heliport space with my luggage. There were men everywhere, checking in, sitting around reading, chatting to their mates or just waiting for their call. One of the men, Phil, jokingly said that I would have to pay excess baggage. The men usually have one travel bag unlike my four: camera and drawing equipment, clothes and Talisman offshore gear bag.

The helicopter was noisy and shaky, as I remembered from previous trips. The pilot told us we would land on Saltire first and suddenly we could see the platform: a surreal, futuristic image in distorted perspective, the unnatural colours of the metallic hard shapes which make up the platform, the derrick and cranes soaring up, containers, the platform's different levels, all crammed into this tight square space sitting above the vast expanse of the North Sea. Every detail was vital to the workings of North Sea operations, pure function. Within five minutes two workers had disembarked from the helicopter and then we were up and away and minutes later we were looking down on Piper B.

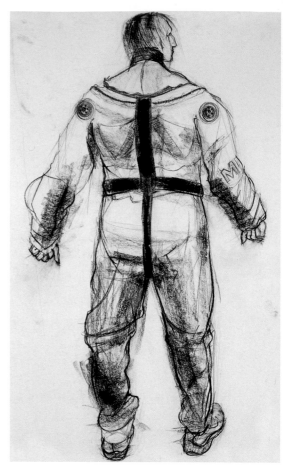

Survival suit figures 2005 conté and charcoal

In the admin. room Tony, the Offshore Installation Manager (OIM), briefed the men on safety matters and working updates, what was happening on the platform including my reason for visiting. After lunch, Ken, the offshore health and safety advisor, showed me a film on safety procedures and emergency evacuation and how to operate various breathing apparatus and evacuation equipment such as the 'doughnut' for abseiling down the platform. We then walked down to the changing rooms where in the minuscule female room I changed into my kit: boiler suit with my name sown into it, steel-cap rigger boots, hard hat, gloves, glasses and ear defenders – the 'green hatter' had arrived.

Ken took me on a walk around the different levels of the platform to help familiarise myself with the layout. Everywhere one was very aware of safety and emergency escape routes, lifeboats poised at the ready. A supply vessel had come in and as I looked down on it memories of my sailing in Stirling Shipping Company's vessels came back to me: the chaos of gravity on one's feet in rough seas and the awareness that a sea-faring vessel was a very different working environment to that of a noisy, almost motionless platform. Ken pointed out Tartan, Claymore and Saltire platforms and the Ocean Princess oil rig in the distance operating in the Piper field.

We walked around to the north side of the platform on the drilling deck side and Ken pointed out the Piper Alpha buoy marker. I was shocked how close we were to the original site of Piper Alpha platform, only 600 metres away. Nothing remains of it; most of the sub-sea leg structure was taken away. I was numb in every sense and all the pain of the aftermath flooded back. My thoughts were drawn to the families and survivors I had got to know. How lonely and desolate the marker looked bobbing and swaying on the surface of the rough grey sea. The reality of that horror struck me full in the face. We moved on.

Above & below The artist at work. PHOTOS: ROBERT POGSON (EXCEPT BOTTOM LEFT, INFRARED IMAGE BY THE ARTIST)

I went back inside to get my sketchpads and drawing equipment. I remembered it was no easy task if you forgot something from the accommodation module. Not only did you have to change out of your work gear before going inside but there were many stairways to climb up and down too, six levels on the platform and two stairways to each level. On the way out onto the enclosed stairway from the accommodation module I passed two guys in William Wilson red boiler suits. We got talking and it turned out that the older man, Bob Simpson, an electrical technician, had worked on Piper Alpha and had known Bob Ballantyne, one of the Piper Alpha survivors, who tragically died of cancer earlier that year.

Outside Ken found a chair for me to sit on and I drew one of the lifeboats jutting out from the platform. I felt very odd, sitting drawing on Piper B on a pleasant September day out in the North Sea.

Back inside I changed and walked up to the personnel offices where Tony, Ken, Sandy the medic and Mike were finishing off their daily afternoon management meeting. I settled myself into a little office and started to write down some ideas and thoughts and look at my drawing. At 5.30 pm we went down to the canteen. Over dinner we talked about Piper Alpha, where Ken and Tony had both worked. Tony especially spoke of many men he knew who were killed that night. He had lost his best mate, Allan Wicks. Ken kept his thoughts to himself.

Ken and I went out at 7 pm so that I could take photographs. It was drizzling but I wanted to take a shot of the large Piper B lettering on the heli-deck. When it started to rain properly we came back inside to the control room where Phil and his team were on night duty. Phil showed me the complexities of the monitor screens' diagrams: wells, gases, separation gases, water, and oil – all beyond my comprehension.

Phil and Ken told me that a school of Porbeagle sharks, between six and eight feet long, had been seen close to the platform in July. They also talked about the beautiful night skies and especially the spectacular *aurora borealis*. Phil said he would love to switch off all the lights on the platform so he could see the sky properly one night. There is no darkness on the platform; everything is lit up with tungsten light. We left Phil to his night shift and I returned to my very comfortable cabin which was furnished with a desk, cupboards, shower, toilet, and television. I found it difficult to get to sleep in the air-conditioned pressurised cabin.

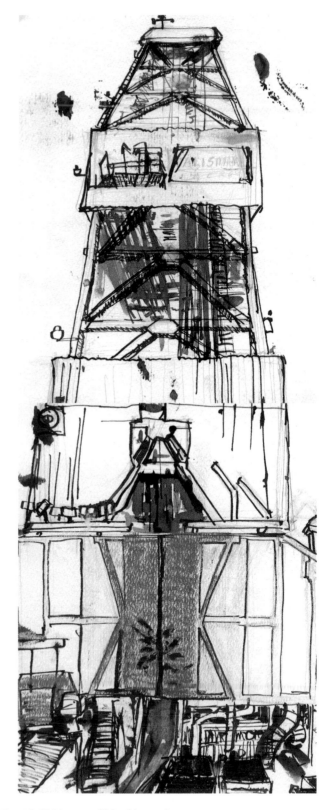

Derrick 2004 pen and ink with pastel

Men at work, Piper Bravo Platform.
PHOTOS: ROBERT POGSON

Friday, 1 October

After breakfast I collected my drawing equipment, put on my work gear and met up with Ken. We made our way down the stairwell to level one and climbed down to the under-deck by means of an exposed steel stairwell; it was like walking down into the belly of the platform. The only way of accessing either side of the platform at this level was to follow the narrow grid walkways which sat on top of the horizontal steel leg structures. We were surrounded by the echoing noise of the sea waves crashing against the massive steel conductor rods and platform legs below and the vibration of the conductors shuddering and knocking against metal holds on the platform – nature and technology meeting in musical chord.

I wanted to draw one of the main valves. Massive in size and bulbous in shape, these were attached to the conductors which soared up and out of the sea. I tried to concentrate on my drawing but the level of noise and the strangeness of my surroundings made this difficult: the constant awareness of the sea's presence, looking down through the metal grid flooring into its depths and grey colour below; the creaking noises and movement of the metal platform counteracting the sea's forces; my gas monitor with its regular beeping noise reminding me that the air was clear of dangerous levels of gas; the occasional muffled tannoy announcement in the distance and the dual function of my ear defenders keeping my ears warm from the wind whistling past while minimising the deafening noise.

I came back inside to say goodbye to Tony, who was going on his two-week leave. In his large office, the only one with a window, he told me that he had started in the industry as an electrical technician and worked his way up. He reminisced about the 1980s when lots of performers were flown offshore to entertain the workforce. Once on Piper Alpha, Noel Edmonds and the band *The Brotherhood of Man* flew out and stayed overnight. The next day the men had raffled the bed sheets the girls in the band had slept in.

Outside again the weather was overcast but not cold. I felt more confident knowing my way around the different levels and remembering always to hold onto the stair rails with at least one hand because the metal walkways were very slippery. I never felt cold in levels one to five on the platform as the heat from the industrial mechanisms kept me warm. I decided to draw the sea and horizon, grey and rough, leading to one directional horizon point. I moved on and up onto the drilling deck, from where I could look directly up at the massive derrick tower. It was a bit blustery but I found some scaffolding planks, which I could sit on, and laid out all my inks for drawing. The noise was different on this level with four

Main Valve Underdeck 2004 pen and ink with pastel

massive John Brown turbines behind me and the wind whistling all around. Noise is part of the offshore experience and each level has its own sound identity.

In the radio control room, Gordon, the radio operator, thought that I would be interested in listening in to a distress call in the North Sea. The call was from a Norwegian ferry, *Noroa*, travelling between the Faroes and Norway, requesting a helicopter from the Shetlands. I listened into the drama unfolding between the Shetland coastguard and the captain of the vessel. A man of North African descent holding a false Greek passport, who was not allowed entry into the Faeroes or Norway, had escaped from a locked cabin with a life jacket on and was threatening to jump overboard. The rescue helicopter was standing by when the man jumped and the helicopter picked him up – he had a broken arm from the fall. I heard the coastguard say that the shore-side authorities had been alerted and were ready to question the man when he arrived onshore. Gordon said there were many May Day calls in the North Sea which people never hear about unless someone is killed.

Sandy came in and told a few stories about guys getting the DTs from drink. He particularly recalled one man wandering around in the middle of the night stark naked shouting, 'Jean, Jean!'

In the afternoon I went back up to the drilling floor to work further on my drawing of the derrick. It was getting more blustery. The crane was about to do a lift operation and I was given the chance to sit in the crane cabin with John, the driver. I followed him high up two ladders and onto the crane cabin level. He proudly showed me its huge electric crane.

Survival Suit Figure 2005 conté and charcoal

In the cabin I watched how easily he manipulated the controls, moving six containers from different levels and awkward positions on the platform. It felt weird sitting up there, the cabin swinging round high above and over the sea.

After supper I experimented taking shots with infrared film of lifeboats and the Piper beacon flashing its lonely flickering light into the blackness of the night.

Back inside, I went up to visit Gordon in the radio room. Gordon had been in the merchant navy before transferring to the oil industry in 1980. He spoke of the stress involved in being a radio operator with only one man on day shift and no night shift. He had been the first R.O. to set foot on the new Piper B platform in

Sea 2004 PHOTO: ROBERT POGSON

August 1992, setting up the radio control room. He was in contact with all the helicopter flights to and from Piper field and also kept an ear out for distress signals, as this was a busy shipping route. His other duties included organising the DVD and video film entertainment showing on television in all cabins. He talked about his colleague Mike Jennings, a Piper Alpha survivor, who had recently retired. Mike had never talked to him about his experiences until the Cullen enquiry came on television. They used to sit and watch the enquiry and as the newsreels from the time of the disaster flashed on screen, Gordon took courage to ask him what it was like. Mike had recalled the horrific events of the disaster.

Gordon the radio operator 2004. PHOTO: ROBERT POGSON

Sketching on deck. PHOTO: ROBERT POGSON

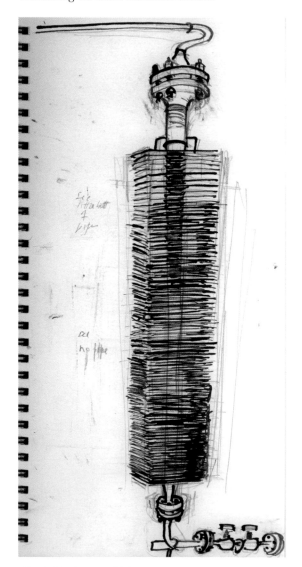
Sketch 2004 pen and ink

With the platform ablaze with fire and explosions, Mike was out on the pipe deck when a man screamed from behind, 'My feet are on fire' and pushed him over the edge, thereby saving his life. Mike went back offshore two weeks after the disaster.

His colleague came in to see if Gordon had finished work and Big John walked in for a chat sucking a lollipop, his trademark. John told us about his recent experience at the world judo championships in Stockholm where his massive Russian opponent had picked him up as if he was a featherweight – John was nineteen stone and a world judo champion many times over. He also recalled how, when he was on Brent Charlie, the contractor's personnel manager had come offshore, collected all the group's employees into one room and brought out reams of paper which turned out to be a £40,000 telephone bill payable to the company. The guys had managed to find a way of phoning their friends and relations all over the world, running up this astronomical bill.

Saturday, 2 October

Got up at 6 am, went down to the canteen for breakfast. My calf muscles ached with going up and down stairways and ladders from the day before. Sandy told me that a flight was due in at 9.45 am; photographer Robert Pogson was coming on board to carry out a series of shots based on my visit.

Outside it was dripping, drizzly rain. It was good to get out in the air and start walking around, looking for details of the structure to draw – air vents, sculptural in their shape to an artist but vital to the workings of the platform. The weather was clearing. There was not a soul about, just the constant deafening noise of the vibrating pipes, valves and pumps. I worked on a drawing of a valve, shaped like a horn, jutting out from the platform.

Inside Ken showed me some digital images of his climb up the derrick crown which were spectacular looking down onto the platform. I felt dizzy just looking at them. I popped in to see Gordon but he was busy on the phones, with all the Saturday papers laid out on his table for the men to collect. Sandy and I went down to the canteen for lunch where Ken was sitting with Robert Pogson and Claire who had also been on the flight. After lunch Robert and I talked briefly about working together and I showed him around the areas of the platform where I was drawing and where he might take photographs.

Ken escorted us to both ends of the lower deck area along the narrow grid walkways and then left us as he had to show around a team of contractors. The platform was busy with contractors on all levels. We came across Big John and Les who were moving a huge cooling tank so that the crane could lift it up. It was a very slow process as the tank's weight was immense and it had to be rolled along and pulled by the chains of a block and tackle. A team of men were moving it and Les, John and scaffolder Brian took it in turns to move the lever on the block and tackle – a very tricky manoeuvre. There was some banter as I tried to draw all the action and Robert took shots on his Hassleblad large format camera.

After dinner, at twilight, we went up onto the heli-deck where Robert took some shots of me drawing, then right down to the under-deck, six levels down, and then to level one where I showed him the Piper Alpha beacon. Back in accommodation, we walked up to the radio room where Gordon was finishing off his work and listening to Robbie Shepherd on BBC Radio Scotland. I started to draw Gordon and Big John came in sucking his lollipop. John had wonderful tattoos on his leg.

Christmas Tree 2005 etching

John Brown Turbines PD4 Piper Bravo 2005 colour etching

Rigger III Piper Field Revisited 2005 colour etching

He told us that he worked out in the gym at 4 am every morning before going on shift and was training to be a masseur. Meanwhile there were lots of phone calls for Gordon from helicopter pilots and from Claymore, Saltire and Tartan platforms. There had been another distress call today, eighteen miles into the Norwegian sector. A fishing boat had accidentally rammed into its sister ship and had gashed it below the water's surface. A pump from the Norwegian beach had been requested but it was too late for the helicopter and they had to abandon ship. They were picked up by a Norwegian vessel.

My legs were aching and I retired to my cabin at 8.30pm.

Sunday, 3 October

I was outside by 7 am and spent the morning drawing. It was a beautiful sunny day and the heat generated from the machines made it very pleasant, apart from the constant noise. A few men passed by and looked to see what I was drawing but it was impossible to have a conversation with the turbines blasting nearby. The flight on which Robert and the contractors were returning to beach had landed and I watched everyone board and the craft fly off and disappear into the distance.

After changing I popped along the corridor to speak to Caroline, one of the field resource team between Piper and Claymore, the only other female working on the platform. Caroline remembered me from UIE shipyard in Clydebank where she had worked in the administration office with Leslie ten years ago. We talked about being

Crane Piper Bravo 2005 colour etching

female on the platform and how she found this work environment. She was now accustomed to it but she sometimes missed the social life at the weekends. Since she had first started working offshore ten years ago there had been a number of changes: a lot less manpower and a lot more work. The social life on the platform had altered: the recent move to televisions in every cabin had destroyed the 'crack'. Once her shift was over she did not go out of her cabin unless there was something special to watch on the big screen down in recreation quarters and she never usually went out of the accommodation module.

Before supper I talked to Claire in her box-cupboard office. Claire was only twenty-five and her role was 'machinery diagnostics conditioning monitoring' on Piper and Claymore. When she first arrived on the platform she had felt vulnerable, particularly with no lock on the cabin, and she used to put a chair in front of the door. She always made a point of saying hello to other women when they came offshore. Her family and fiancé worried about her safety offshore but she now felt very safe and happy in her job.

After supper I went out to take some more night shots with an infrared film. Up on the heli-deck it was so windy I could hardly stand.

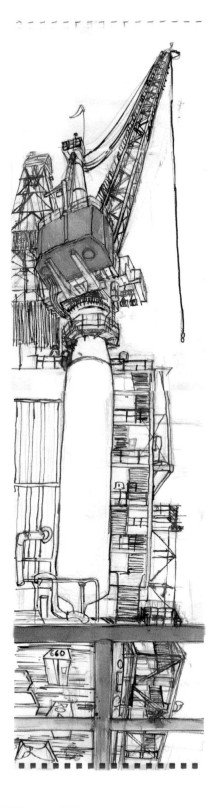

Crane Piper Bravo 2004 pen and ink wash

Sketch 2005 conté and charcoal

I had a morning to finish off everything before the flight which was due in at 12.45 pm. It was miserable outside, pouring rain but no wind. I walked around level one where the Christmas tree area is, very eerie but fascinating. Through the gap of the well holds I could view the sea directly below. After a quick sketch of one of the valves I decided to go six flights up to heli-deck. First though, I walked round to the side where the Piper Alpha beacon was and said my final silent farewell in the rain. Beside me rows of seagulls were quietly perched all the way up the flare tower.

Up on the heli-deck a skein of ducks was flying around.

Back in accommodation a call came for me to go up to the radio room. Gordon told me that Ken was going down to check the spider deck as the abseilers – RATs (Rope Access Technicians) – would be painting part of the platform's leg. This was my chance; I had always wanted to go down to the spider deck. It was still raining and damp as I made my way to the under-deck where I spotted Ken down with the 'rats' getting their gear on, harness, ropes, life jackets; one of the 'rats' was an Aussie. These guys are a fairly new phenomenon in the North Sea oil industry. Previously scaffolders would have had to make platforms for painters to work on the platform legs. Now the work is carried out by climbers who dangle off ropes at precarious angles and heights and carry out paint or repair jobs on the spot.

With a life jacket on I walked down a stairway which was suspended in mid-air leading down to the spider deck. The deck is a narrow metal grid walkway sitting on the horizontal pipe structure of the platform just above sea level. We were so close to the surface of the sea that you felt you could touch it. The towering underbelly of the platform rose above us like gigantic soaring gothic pillars. The standby vessel was near at hand in case of an accident. Ken checked the walkways and grids before we stepped on them, as he had not been down for a while. I took some photographs as there was not enough time to sketch. The wind was getting up so the abseilers would not be there for long.

Survival Suit Figure 2005 conté and charcoal

RAT Robert Ellis 2005 conté and charcoal

Sketches 2005 charcoal, conté and pastel

Survival Suit Figure 2005 conté and charcoal

There was little time left before my flight. I said my goodbyes and made my way to the assembly point where Caroline and seven others were waiting. I could smell the men's aftershave and Caroline looked like another person with her make-up on and her long blond hair loose. It was pouring rain as we stepped outside along the rope-floored heli-deck and into the helicopter. We made a stop over at Saltire where one of the passengers disembarked. During the journey most of the men slept, even amidst the shaking and noise of the moving craft. The skies began to clear as we approached the beach and we followed the coast down from Peterhead to Dyce. Wonderful colours came into view, reminding me of what I had been missing for five days: from the dull grey/blue-green colour offshore to cleaner, light green/blue seas, the beautiful range of rich greens of the land and silver sands of the beaches.

As I waited for the Inverness train I reflected on my visit. The strong emotions evoked in me on revisiting the site of that disaster were very much present. But along with the horror and pity I was feeling, were other more positive thoughts. The present reality of the place had helped me lay to rest a lot of ghosts and was already beginning to provide me with inspiration for future work.

Offshore Flower 2005 colour etching

"I never look out towards the marker and I always hate July."

Piper Bravo worker

From FOR THE UNKNOWN SEAMEN OF THE 1939 – 45 WAR
BURIED IN IONA CHURCHYARD

One would like to be able to write something for them
not for the sake of the writing but because
a man should be named in dying as well as living,
in drowning as well as on death-bed, and because
the brain being brain must try to establish laws.
Yet these events are not amenable
to any discipline that we can impose
and are not in the end even imaginable.

Best not to make much of it and leave these seamen
in the equally altering acre they now have
inherited from strangers though yet human.
They fell from sea to earth from grave to grave
and, griefless now, taught others how to grieve.

Iain Crichton Smith, 1959

Opposite
Piper Alpha Marker
at night 2004.
PHOTO: ROBERT POGSON

SUE JANE TAYLOR A CRITICAL INTRODUCTION

Between 1984 and 1994, the artist Sue Jane Taylor recorded the life, onshore and offshore, of men involved in the oil industry in Scotland. This essay sets Taylor's work in the context of Scottish art and, more widely, the history of art as it relates to human beings involved, often in extremis, in hard manual and physical labour.

Scottish art falls, by and large, into the category of the genteel, epitomised by the *belle peinture* of the mid-twentieth-century Edinburgh School which dominated ways of seeing Scotland and its landscape. But running parallel to this world of landscape, seascape and still-life is a different vein. Scotland industrialised early; its reserves of coal, iron, labour and its developing communications infrastructure encouraged a rapid urban expansion in the nineteenth century when traditional 'heavy' industries such as coal mining, ship-building and foundry-work reached their peak.

The advent of the First World War led to even heavier industrial activity, in particular on the Clyde, where massive man-power and resources went into the construction of some of the biggest engineering structures the world has ever seen. Muirhead Bone (1876–1953) recorded Glasgow's late-nineteenth-century expansion and its continuing activity during the 1914–18 war. The etchings 'Cranes: Start of a New Ship' (1917) and 'A Shipyard Scene from a Big Crane', of the same year, are typical examples of Bone's work at this time. They show the energy and activity of a working shipyard where the workers are dwarfed by the sheer size of the structures they are toiling to complete.

Other artists, too, have worked in this tradition. Around the time Bone was working in Glasgow as a war artist, John Duncan Fergusson (1871–1961) spent six weeks in 1918 painting in Portsmouth Docks. Earlier still, William Bell Scott (1811–1890) had depicted industrial Britain in such works as 'Iron and Coal' (1861), popular in part because of the relative rarity of its subject matter.

Opposite
Artist in her studio, Stockholm 1985.
PHOTO: ETIENNE GAMELON

It should also be remembered that one of the most talented painters to have emerged from Scotland in the past twenty years, Steven Campbell, was employed as a steel-works maintenance engineer for seven years prior to entering Glasgow School of Art. Like Stanley Spencer before him, Campbell invests the imagery of the shipyard with religious and spiritual metaphor. Other Scottish-based artists, in particular Kate Downie, have delighted in depicting with verve and passion the glories of Scotland's engineering.

But it is perhaps to the English painter Stanley Spencer rather than to Bone that we should look in establishing a precedent for Taylor's vision. Spencer was assigned the task of recording the life and work of the Lithgow shipyards at Port Glasgow during the Second World War and his work as an official war artist was the subject of a major exhibition in Glasgow in 1994 and another in Edinburgh in 1999. Spencer made himself a part of this world; his work identifies with the working men and women he represents in his stylised but oddly realist images. Spencer, as an educated middle-class, diminutive southern English intellectual, made himself at home and was accepted and admired in an environment diametrically opposed to his own: so too did Taylor, as a young woman, in a threatening, at times hostile and frightening male environment, make herself at home, and also ultimately found acceptance.

There was, perhaps, an inevitability to Taylor's decision to depict the life and images on the various oil-related installations she visited during the 1980s, due in part to growing up on the Black Isle, a part of Scotland greatly affected, both physically and economically, by the developing oil industry. For a young, visually aware person growing up in such an environment, the effect of the physical changes and interventions on the landscape must have been enormous. One can imagine in Taylor an admixture of fascination and trepidation, gazing at the vast male-built, man-inhabited world represented by the colossal structures of the oil industry. Taylor admits, too, a kind of quasi-eroticism in her attraction to this world of men, machinery, steel and flame.

Taylor trained at Gray's School of Art, Aberdeen and followed this with post-graduate studies at the Slade School of Fine Art, London. Gray's was a natural choice for a young, gifted artist from the Highlands of Scotland. At Gray's she was taught design by Fred Stiven and Ainslie Yule, drawing by Frances Walker, painting by Joyce Cairns and, later, printmaking by Gordon Bryce. This was a liberal curriculum allowing breadth, depth and scope for personal experimentation. It is difficult to exaggerate the effect of such training on a young artist; these teachers were part of a continuing tradition in Scottish art where the crafts of drawing and painting were allied strongly to observational and compositional skills. It is no exaggeration to state that in Scotland, the links between this kind of approach and the world of mathematics (in particular geometry), architecture, design and engineering were exceptionally strong. From these teachers Taylor learned important basic skills: she cites the 'golden mean' and the fundamentals underlying the practice of modern masters such as Le Corbusier as being highly significant. An understanding of the principles involved in design and engineering is fundamental to Taylor's ability to render them convincing in print and drawing. She has stated that the craft of drawing and representation is central to her approach. Her awareness is obvious when considering not only her depictions of man-made structures but also, importantly, the human form.

When Taylor moved, at the age of twenty-one, to study for a post-graduate diploma at the Slade she recalls a vibrant cosmopolitan atmosphere with an exciting city to explore. At the Slade, Taylor studied printmaking under Bartolomeu Dos Santos, a powerful personality and an inspiring teacher. Significantly, Taylor recalls the late Sir Eduardo Paolozzi in his capacity not as a teacher but as external assessor: 'I will never forget his amazing, big sculptural hands – just like his own sculptures – and his huge, solid, strong head resting on this massive strong body.'[1]

As Taylor became more involved in the subject of the oil-worker she wanted to look into how other visual artists portrayed the theme of the worker, particularly in more recent art history. Courbet, Millet and Gauguin were obvious artists to look at, as their work ranged from romantic subjects, such as peasants in the fields, to a brutal and much starker reality. Perhaps rather more surprisingly the inter-war German artist, Kathe Kollwitz provided an influence not only through her 'powerful portrait studies but also her agility and natural ability to transfer these skills to etching and lithography. And her observation of the marked, scarred faces of the toils of poverty and working life at that time.'[2] Taylor also cites the eighteenth-century Italian printmaker, Giambattista Piranesi, as a powerful model, in particular, 'his incredible, fantastical images of imaginary prisons ... creating such powerful towering structures in the form of the etched line '.[3]

The list of influences on Taylor is as broad as it is deep. Another is Joan Eardley who, like Taylor, worked for part of her career on Clydeside but moved to more peaceful conditions in the north of Scotland. Eardley was transfixed by the influence of the sea and her habit of working *en plein air* obviously appeals to Taylor.

Another influence is Glasgow artist Ken Currie, notably for his work 'The Glasgow History Mural', commissioned by the People's Palace Museum, Glasgow, in 1987: eight large-scale painted panels commemorating the 200th anniversary of the Carlton Weaver Massacre. 'Conviction and passion shine through in these works and breathe new life into an old tradition.'[4]

Taylor also admires Turner for his 'free style of painting watercolour from the open air, expressive and experimental for his time. His method and way of recording and experiencing the natural elements ... such as strapping himself to a mast in extreme rough weather out at sea.'[5]

As a student at the Slade, Taylor became fascinated by the concept of 'The Northern Landscape'. In 1984 she was awarded the Swedish Institute one-year scholarship to study at the Konsthogskolan in Stockholm. The Norwegian Edvard Munch in particular had a deep influence and there is a clear thematic association with Taylor's work, as was demonstrated in a touring exhibition 'Munch and the Workers', which was shown at The City Art Centre in Edinburgh in 1985 and included not only depictions of agricultural and agrarian labour but workers in an urban setting undertaking constructional labour. [6]

In all of these cases, and in Taylor's, there is an important dimension: that of empathy with the worker and identification with him, as if he and the artist were involved in some communal project linked by work.

The body of work contained within the time period under discussion (1984–94) is large by any standards, amounting to over 400 photographs, drawings, prints, paintings and sculptures. I have outlined above the context of the work and will now consider in detail a few images, linking them to a general theme.

'The Oil Man and the Stag' (1989)

This etching, completed in 1989, represents the Scottish oil industry in allegorical as well as literal terms. The image of a sardonic worker in blue hard hat and spotted kerchief is juxtaposed with the head and antlers of the stag. To one side is a dark windblown tree. The work relates to a number of others completed at this time, including 'Crann Dubh' (Black Tree), which shows a woman and a man in proximity to another lone, dark outlined skeletal tree.

The motif of the stag (well known from the kitsch of Landseer to the politicised, socialist polemic of McGrath) might symbolise Scotland but, as with the tree, it stands for the much more general and fragile concept of nature, pitted against humanity's need for work, wealth, fuel and profit; here old and new, industrial and organic, clash in a seemingly intractable opposition. As well as invoking such powerful symbolism and all its attendant allusions, Taylor pictures her worker as identifiable, with a face. This is her habitual approach and suggests empathy, understanding and her compassionate need to represent the 'human face' of technological progress.

'Rigger 1' (1987)

This etching, dating from 1987, is more iconic and thus more generic than 'The Oil Man and the Stag' and is a deceptively simple yet arresting image. It shows the head and upper torso of a rigger clad in a hooded red protective suit. Although identifiable, the noble face with its straight nose and thick moustache recalls Romantic imagery of the warrior or adventurer.

As if to emphasise the nobility of this warrior pose, the harness attachments on the rigger's survival suit are deliberately blurred, assuming the role of ornamental buckles or even brooches on the plaids of medieval Scottish Highland chiefs. Although the colour scheme here is simple – red and black – the way in which it has been employed shows not only an assured compositional sense, but also the effect of colour on the senses. For here, the red of the survival suit is allowed to 'bleed' beyond the confines of the etched outline of the figure, expressively suggesting movement and emotion.

This study relates directly to Taylor's fascination with Munch who used colour in a similarly symbolic way, in particular in his series of 'jealousy' paintings.

Studies For 'Kromer Hat' (1993)

Taylor first visited John Brown's shipyard (now UIE) on Clydebank in September 1987. Although the old cloth 'bunnets' so vividly and memorably depicted by Stanley Spencer have long since vanished, ousted by health and safety regulations, and been replaced by the hard hat, the humour and individuality – the humanity – of these men is asserted in the form of differently coloured hats for different trades. The Kromer Hat came over from Milwaukee, primarily as a safety item. However, as well as the safety aspects, they come in a variety of patterns and colours.

Above The artist's studio, Noo. 19 Cataibh, Dornoch PHOTO: FIN MACRAE

This, coupled with the colourful array of bandanas, inspired the title of Taylor's 1993 project which culminated in the unveiling of the 'Kromer Hat' worker's head 'presented to the people of Clydebank'. Although the head was modelled on Roy Callaghan, one of the welders, there is as well as this distinctive acknowledgment of humanity, a dedication to all workers from this industry, and beyond.

Such complexity underpins Taylor's approach and typifies her bold and uncompromising stance, born of understanding, empathy, craft and a highly defined artistry.

Giles Sutherland
Edinburgh 2005

[1] Taylor, S.J letter to Giles Sutherland, 26 September 2002
[2] ibid.
[3] ibid.
[4] 'Vigorous Imagination' exhibition catalogue, National Galleries of Scotland 1987
[5] Taylor, S.J letter to Giles Sutherland, 26 September 2002
[6] Taylor's touring exhibition 'Oil Worker Scotland' was itself shown here in 1989

SUE JANE TAYLOR SELECTED WORKS

Looking up at Sante Fe 140 1984	colour etching	980mm x 500mm edition /20	2
The Stirling Teal Boys 1984	colour etching	600mm x 770mm edition /20	3
Aberdeen Harbour 1984	colour etching	980mm x 500mm edition /20	4
Security Guards 1986	colour etching with chine collé	800mm x 590mm edition /10	11
Knock Out Tank 1986 (detail)	pen and ink wash	570mm x 790mm	11
Robbie, Flotta 1987	colour etching with chine collé	590mm x 820mm edition /10	13
Orkney Landscape I 1984	colour etching	550mm x 550mm edition /8	16
Mrs Sinclair 1987	mixed media on paper	1080mm x 1700mm	17
Orkney Landscape II 1984	colour etching	550mm x 550mm edition /8	18
Orkney Landscape III 1984	colour etching	400mm x 250mm edition /20	21
Boys of the North 1986	mixed media on paper	1080mm x 1560mm	25
Shop One 1988	mixed media on paper	510mm x 750mm	29
Shop Two 1988	mixed media on paper	780mm x 560mm	30
Tree of Gold, Milnafua 1988	graphite and gold pigment	A6	34
Niggers of the North 1988	pastel and graphite	A5	35
Tea Time at Kishorn 1986	colour etching with chine collé	590mm x 790mm edition /10	40
Worker, Total Module 1986	mixed media on paper	1080mm x 750mm	45
St Fergus 1991	mixed media on paper	1390mm x 780mm	52
Rob at his Desk 1987	mixed media on paper	640mm x 840mm	56
Waiting for the Call I 1987	mixed media on paper	1080mm x 750mm	61
Fisherman I 1991	conté and charcoal	750mm x 540mm	62
Tea Time Offshore 1987	colour etching with chine collé	890mm x 600mm edition /10	63
Waiting for the Call II 1987	colour etching with chine collé	590mm x 790mm edition /10	67
Oilworker 1989	colour etching	700mm x 2000 edition /10	78–79
Oilman and the Stag 1989	colour etching with chine collé	770mm x 980mm edition /10	80
John, Welder at Arnish 1988	acrylic on board	700mm x 1000mm	89
Fisherman II 1991	conté and charcoal	1080mm x 750mm	90
Islander 1988	mixed media on paper	1080mm x 400mm	93

Tony the Chef 1988	mixed media on paper	9000mm x 9000mm	100
Bond Shop Man 1988	conté and charcoal	700mm x 1000mm	103
Block and Tackles 1989	conté and charcoal	600mm x 770mm	108
Piper Alpha Crane 1987	pen and ink wash with pastel	760mm x 650mm	108
Rigger II 1987	colour etching	460mm x 750mm edition /8	109
John the Electrician 1988	mixed media on paper	400mm x 1400mm	110
Rigger I 1987	colour etching	550mm x 740mm edition /8	112
Good News at Clydebank 1993	colour etching	970mm x 740mm edition /10	117
Untitled 1993	acrylic on paper	500mm x 1000mm	120
Kromer Hat 1993	charcoal and conté with found objects from workshop floor	700mm x1000mm	121
Man with Bunnet 1993	charcoal	A6	122
Kromer Hat 1993	cast bronze and riveted iron plinth	700mm x 500mm x 3000mm	125
Roy's Bandana 1992	mixed media and found objects from the workshop floor	600mm x450mm	126
Dave's Stove 1988	conté and pastel	780mm x 550mm	130
Laurie's Catch 1989	colour etching with chine collé	300mm x 900mm edition /10	131
Angus 1989	colour etching with chine collé	460mm x 980mm edition /10	132
Approaching the Rig 1985	colour etching	490mm x 990mm A/P 1	134
Rough Seas II 1985	colour etching	980mm x 790mm A/P 1	135
Untitled 1989	mixed media with gold pigment	570mm x 790mm	136
Sea of Gold 1989	mixed media with gold pigment	250mm x 400mm	142
Rough Seas III 1985	Etching	490mm x 980mm A/P 1	146
An Crann Dubh (The Black Tree) 1989	colour etching	880mm x 590mm edition /1	151
James MacMillan, Glasgow 1992	conté and pastel	300mm x 600mm	164
Piper Alpha Memorial	bronze with gold leaf	4000mm x 1830mm x 1830mm	166
Survival suit figures 2005	conté and charcoal	540mm x 750mm	170–71
Christmas Tree 2005	etching	250mm x 800mm edition /8	179
John Brown Turbines PD4 Piper Bravo 2005	colour etching	550mm x 600mm edition /8	180
Rigger III Piper Field Revisited 2005	colour etching	420mm x 800mm edition /8	181
Crane Piper Bravo 2004	colour etching	250mm x 800mm edition /8	183
RAT Robert Ellis 2005	conté and charcoal	550mm x 1200mm	186
Offshore Flower 2005	colour etching	390mm x 390mm edition /8	189

INDEX

Text Acknowledgements

Kenneth MacKenzie translated excerpts from 'Moladh na Luinge' ('The Praise of the Ship') and Alastair mac Mhaighstir Alastair 'Birlinn Chlann Raghnaill ('The Galley of Clan Ranald') from *An Lasair* (Birlinn, 2001) reproduced by permission of Ronald Black; Norman MacCaig 'Construction Site' reproduced by permission of Polygon, an imprint of Birlinn Ltd; Iain Crichton Smith 'Between Sea and Moor' (from *As I Remember: Ten Scottish Authors Recall How Writing began for Them*, ed. Maurice Lindsay) and 'For the Unknown Seamen of the 1939–1945 War Buried in Iona Churchyard' reproduced by permission of Carcanet Press; Edwin Morgan excerpt from 'Glasgow Sonnets' reproduced by permission of Carcanet Press; Ken Morrice 'Caul Kail' from *For All I Know* (Aberdeen University Press, 1981) and 'Boom Toon' from *Relations* (Rainbow Books, 1979) reproduced by permission of Norah Morrice; Helen Cruickshank 'Overdue' (from *Up the Noran Water*, Methuen 1934) reproduced by permission of Alfred Hunter; George Campbell Hay excerpt from 'Seeker, Reaper', reproduced by kind permission of the Lorimer Trust and taken from *Collected Poems and Songs of George Campbell Hay*, ed. Michel Byrne (Edinburgh University Press, 2002); George Gunn 'Remembering Magnus' and 'Derrick Man' reproduced by permission of the author; Robin Robertson 'Aberdeen' from *A Painted Field* (Macmillan, 1997) reproduced by permission of Macmillan, London, UK.

Photographers' Acknowledgements:

Etienne Gamelon; Fin MacCrae; Murdo MacLeod; Gunnie Moberg; Robert Pogson; Bill Russell; Ray Smith.